"This Dreadful Visitation"

THE FAMINE IN LURGAN/PORTADOWN

Gerard Mac Atasney
with foreword by
Christine Kinealy

First published in 1997
by
Beyond the Pale Publications
PO Box 337
Belfast BT9 7BT
Tel: +44 (0)1232 431170
Fax: +44 (0)1232 301299
E-mail: btpale@unite.co.uk
Internet site: http://www.unite.net/customers/btp/

British Library Cataloguing-in-Publication Data.
A catalogue record for this book is available from the British Library.

ISBN 1-900960-02-8

Printed by
Colour Books Ltd, Dublin

For my mother and father

The Irish Labourers' 'Pater Noster'

Give us this day our daily bread,
Father in mercy hear our prayer,
All hope in human aid is fled,
We sink in deep despair.

Our little ones scream out with pain,
And clamour to be fed,
Father, they cry to us in vain,
Give us our daily bread.

O'er the gaunt infant at the breast,
The mother bows her head,
The fount is dry, in vain 'tis prest,
Give us our daily bread.

Our eldest born, with hollow eye,
And eager stealthy tread,
Would take the food we cannot buy,
Give us our daily bread.

We must not beg, *he* shall not steal,
Though stores before us spread,
But we will work with earnest zeal,
Give us our daily bread.

Famine hath laid her withering hand
Upon each little head,
O Christ! is this a Christian land?
Give us our daily bread.

Thy will be done, Father receive
Our souls when we are dead,
In Heaven we shall not pine and grieve,
Or want our daily bread.

The Belfast Vindicator, 1847

Contents

ACKNOWLEDGEMENTS

I wish to express my gratitude to the following for their help:

Dr. Christine Kinealy for writing the foreword to this book; Dr. Michael Kennedy, Department of Modern History, Queen's University, for his invaluable critical analysis; the Archivists of the National Archive, Dublin, especially Donal Moore; Woolsey Gracey, Shankill Parish Church; Rob Goodbody and Karel Kiely for their help with Quaker sources; Elizabeth Mullin; Roddy Hegarty; Arthur Chapman; Dr. John Dallat, University of Ulster; Trevor McCavery; Mary Delargy, Linen Hall Library; Mary McVeigh and Joe Canning, Armagh Library Headquarters; Dr. Greer Ramsey and Catherine McCullough, Armagh County Museum; Sean Harte, Caretaker, Lurgan Hospital; Oliver Burns;.

Thanks are due to the following for kind permission to reproduce photographs and archive documents:

The Deputy Keeper of Records, Public Records Office, Northern Ireland; National Archives, Dublin; the Vestries of the Church of Ireland Congregations of Shankill, Seagoe, Tullylish, and Glendermott; Sean Sexton.

My special thanks go to Dr. Bill Crawford, Federation for Ulster Local Studies, who shared his unrivalled knowledge of the sources with me; Dr. Ian Maxwell, Public Records Office, Belfast, whose great generosity and diligence meant that many vital sources were brought to my attention; Philip Wilson, Curator, Craigavon Museum Project, for help in all aspects of the research; and Daphne Abernethy for help with the index.

Lastly, my thanks to my mother and father for their continued encouragement and support.

Gerard Mac Atasney
Lurgan, March 1997

List of Tables

List of Figures

Foreword

A remarkable feature of the Irish Famine of 1845-52 is that until recently it has attracted so little attention from historians. The 150th anniversary has created a renewed interest in the event, resulting in a new body of research. More has been written about the Famine in the last few years than was written in the previous century and a half. As a consequence, a more textured and nuanced view of the Famine is emerging. However, much research still remains to be undertaken, especially at the local level where the human consequences of the tragedy had most impact.

Gerard Mac Atasney's study of the Famine in the Lurgan/ Portadown area will make a significant contribution to Famine historiography. He has used sources from both local and national archives, together with his own knowledge of the region, to build up a comprehensive and fascinating picture of the impact of the Famine in that area. His conclusions provide compelling evidence that there was a Famine in Ulster.

On the eve of the Famine, County Armagh was one of the most commercially successful linen-producing areas, not only in Ireland, but in the world. In the preceding decades, however, the domestic linen industry had undergone a period of economic adjustment and technological transformation. As a consequence, the standard of living of many weavers had declined and their income was precarious. Moreover, there was a large group of people who did not have access to the alternative source of income provided by weaving but who subsisted on agriculture. Like their counterparts in the West of Ireland, they relied on potatoes for the bulk of their diet. The destruction of the potato crop in 1845 and subsequent years left these people without food.

This study demonstrates that the situation of the destitute in County Armagh had much in common with the suffering of the poor in the west of Ireland. Evictions, emigration, disease and, the most dramatic indicator of all, mortality, were all high in Armagh, especially amongst the poorest groups. The value of a local research is evident in Gerard Mac Atasney's study of mortality in the Lurgan workhouse. He demonstrates that in 1847 more Protestants than Catholics died in the workhouse, which is a valuable reminder that poverty was apparent in all denominations. Moreover, the examination of the administration of the Lurgan workhouse illustrates that poor management, incompetent masters, indifferent Guardians and financial problems were not confined to the poorest Unions in the West of Ireland. However, the rate-in-aid debate in 1849 – when many northern Unions objected to paying an additional tax for redistribution to some of the western Unions – contributed to the myth that the Unions in the north of the country had managed their affairs better than those situated elsewhere.

Gerard Mac Atasney's fine local study will force a re-evaluation of the impact of the Famine in Ireland. He demonstrates that the Famine also took place in Ulster and that destitution and excess mortality existed in the heart of Ireland's major industrial region.

Christine Kinealy
Liverpool, March 1997

Christine Kinealy is a Fellow of the University of Liverpool. She is author of *This Great Calamity: the Irish Famine 1845-52* (Gill and Macmillan, 1994) and *A Death-Dealing Famine: the Great Hunger in Ireland* (Pluto Press, 1997).

Chronology

1845

September

Potato blight strikes for first time; approximately one third of crop lost.

1846

March

Potatoes replaced by meal, then Indian meal, in workhouse diet.

May

Outbreak of fever in workhouse warrants investigation by Central Board of Health. They advise the Board of Guardians to dismiss the Medical Officer; this is refused.

August/September

Potato crop fails again; eighty to ninety per cent of crop lost.

November

Duke of Manchester and Lord Lurgan initiate land drainage schemes as relief work.

December

Petition from Portadown to Lord John Russell requesting an Extraordinary Presentment Session to provide work for the distressed.

Workhouse filled to capacity (800).

1847

January

Fever rampant in workhouse; mortality level is highest in Ulster.

Ten Relief Committees formed throughout the Union.

February

Workhouse deaths reach a peak of 95 for week ending February 6.

March

Inquiry into condition of workhouse by Dr. Smith of the Board of Health. Internal investigation prompted by the Rev. Oulton into standard of workhouse food.

Coordinated attacks on barges containing food near Portadown.

April

Resignation of workhouse medical officer; dismissal of master.

Death of Lord Lurgan from typhus fever.

May

Temporary fever hospitals established throughout the Union. Camp hospital sited opposite workhouse.

Introduction of government-sponsored soup kitchens under the Temporary Relief Act.

August

Poor Law Extension Act sees local Relief committees wound up. Poor relief now the responsibility of each Union.

Workhouse graveyard filled to capacity. All burials moved to Shankill parish burial ground.

September

Union reported to be in serious financial difficulty.

December

Greer's Distillery in the Back Lane, Lurgan, obtained as auxiliary workhouse.

1848

March

New graveyard opened on workhouse grounds.

May

Young Ireland Rebellion; some support in Lurgan area.

1849

March

Outbreak of cholera in Lurgan and Portadown.

Huge anti-Rate-in-Aid rally in Lurgan.

September

Cholera epidemic ends.

Reintroduction of potatoes into workhouse diet.

Introduction

The spectacle of a bankrupt union with a horde of starving paupers, and a ruined peasantry on the brink of pauperism, has not yet been seen in Ulster.

The *Belfast News Letter*, 23 March 1849.

North-east Ulster escaped relatively lightly from the Great Famine.[1]

Philip Ollerenshaw, 1985.

In 1840 the Lurgan Union workhouse was built ... but the town seems to have been spared the calamities that make the Famine Year so tragic a memory.[2]

T.G.F. Patterson, 1975.

The three statements above, selected from many, have helped perpetuate one of the greatest myths of modern Irish history, namely, that the Great Famine did not affect Ulster. Each derives its rationale from assumptions based on social, political and historiographical factors which ensured that the study of the Famine in Ulster became a misnomer. An examination of these factors is essential in order to explain such thinking.

From the day they were first constructed, workhouses were dreaded by most of the population. They were huge, grim buildings, designed to deter all but the truly destitute from entering. To a large degree, they succeeded in this aim until the mid-1840s, when the Famine struck. With nowhere else to go, the poor pleaded in their thousands for entry, in the hope of obtaining food and shelter. However, with so many people in close confinement, disease spread and, as a consequence, the workhouses became synonymous with disease and death.

Thus, in the years that followed, the workhouse was not only viewed as being an inhospitable building, it was also regarded as somewhere that you went to as a last resort, usually never to return.

In the North of Ireland, this belief was reinforced well into the twentieth century by the fact that the Poor Law remained on the statute book until the introduction of the national health service in 1948. Hence, what in later years were regarded by many as hospitals were still remembered by older generations as workhouses. Indeed, many of today's hospitals, including that in Lurgan, were constructed from renovations of the original workhouses. Given that memories of the workhouse invariably involved much sadness, it is understandable that many people would wish to forget them. While commemorating the death of a father or grandfather in battle is a source of much pride to later generations, the same cannot be said of a relative who died in the workhouse. Even today, when workhouse records are open for consultation, some family researchers refuse to use them, such is the stigma associated with the buildings.

The fact that the north-east was the most industrially advanced region of the country gave carte blanche to those who wished to portray it as somehow ethnically superior. The *Belfast News Letter* editorial, quoted above, is one example; many others are quoted in Chapter 8. Inherent in such comments was the belief that Ulster held a quasi-racial, cultural and religious superiority over the rest of the country. Of course, the local gentry peddled such notions as a means of promoting their own interests while at the same time denigrating the suffering of their fellow Irishmen and women.

This notion of somehow being 'different' was reinforced by the partition of the country. It encouraged such thinking as the refusal in 1936 of the Stormont government to allow schools to participate in an all-Ireland project involving interviews with grandparents about their memories of the Famine. Aside from the political difficulties of dealing with De Valera's Free State government on such a matter, the Stormont regime rejected it for other reasons. Firstly, in their view, famine history was just another nationalist stick with which to beat the British. Secondly, in trying to emphasise the independence of the new northern state, any initiative involving an all-Ireland perspective would have been the last thing they wished to promote.

While political machinations may be understood, even if not justified, what is not acceptable is the connivance of those writing history. In October 1995 at one of a series of lectures on the Famine organised by the Linen Hall Library, Professor Mary Daly of University College Dublin stated:

> Now that we are in a ceasefire situation, we can talk about aspects of history which we may previously have felt uncomfortable with.

This notion of writing 'safe' history within clearly defined guidelines appears to have been policy for those writing about the history of Ulster. The National Archives in Dublin contain thousands of documents relating to the Famine in this part of the island, yet it was not until Jonathan Bardon produced his seminal *A History of Ulster* in 1992 that a serious attempt was made to analyse the effects of the catastrophe here. Colle's four volume *A History of Ulster* devotes two pages to the Famine, while the official history of the Orange Order, covering a period of 150 years in two volumes, does not mention it at all.

Another aspect of historiography which has helped foster a myth centres around the nationalist-revisionist debate, to the virtual exclusion of other possibilities.

One of the earliest exponents of the nationalist version of the Famine was John Mitchel. Blaming both the British government and absentee landlords, he argued that the Famine was an act of genocide by those who, engendered with a racial hatred of the Irish, used it to devastate the population, both economically and politically. For Mitchel the most striking symbol of this campaign was the export of foodstuffs from Irish ports while starving people watched the ships depart.

The revisionists have, in their opinion, sought to counterbalance the 'excesses' of Mitchel by destroying the traditional nationalist viewpoint and replacing it with a supposedly objective, value-free history. Thus, in such writings the effect of the Famine as a watershed is questioned and stress is laid upon pre-Famine demographic and land tenure changes. The level of mortality is revised downwards and the attitudes of landlords are reassessed.

The consequence of all of this is that historians usually side with one or other of the ideologies, to the detriment of other aspects of the subject. Hence, in Kinealy's words:

> Famine historiography has been polarised within the confines of a concentric and narrow historical discourse. A false but emotionally powerful dichotomy has been created between traditional, reactionary nationalist and secular, modern revisionism.[3]

Thus social aversion, political expediency and historiographical avoidance have ensured that the study of the Famine in Ulster was not a subject for 'real' historians.

This book offers an in-depth investigation into the lives of the people of North Armagh, South-west Antrim and North-west Down, areas which were amalgamated under the Poor Law Act of 1838 to become the Lurgan Poor Law Union. This region was the centre of the Ulster 'linen belt' and as such should have been best able to withstand the ravages of the Famine. As the book illustrates, however, conditions in the latter part of 1846 and early months of 1847 were as severe here as in any other part of the country. Utilising previously ignored sources, a picture is drawn of an area that suffered greatly during the Famine, particularly with regard to the number of fatalities.

As well as exploding the myth that the Famine never happened in the North-east, the point is also made that the vast majority of those who died, both inside and outside the workhouse, were Protestants.

Footnotes

1. P. Ollerenshaw, 'Industry, 1820-1914', in L. Kennedy and P. Ollerenshaw (eds), *An Economic History of Ulster, 1820-1939*, Manchester University Press 1985, p. 74.
2. T.G.F. Patterson, 'The Town of Lurgan', in E. Estyn Evans (ed), *Harvest Home – the Last Sheaf: a Selection from the Writings of T.G.F. Patterson*, Dundalgan Press, Dundalk, 1975, p. 122.
3. Christine Kinealy, 'Beyond Revisionism – reassessing the Great Irish Famine', *History Ireland*, 3(4), 1995.

1.

Workhouses and the Poor Law

Everybody admits that a provision for the poor is necessary
but scarcely two agree as to how that provision is to be made.[1]

This statement by Colonel William Blacker, a member of the
local gentry and future chairman of Lurgan Union Board of
Guardians, encapsulated the difficulty faced by those with the
responsibility for framing a system to alleviate the chronic poverty
and destitution then widespread in nineteenth century Ireland.
The eventual solution, the Irish Poor Law, would be judged by
many in future years by its ability to cope with one of the greatest
disasters in this or any other country – the Great Famine of the
1840s.

Prior to 1838 the poor in Ireland were assisted almost totally
by private charity. Locally, this usually consisted of weekly
voluntary collections from churches. In 1827 the Church of
Ireland in Drumcree elected a committee of 21 parishioners to
ensure adequate provision for the poor of the area. Having
established that there were 39 beggars in the parish, copper badges
were supplied to each of them as a means of identification. They
were then fed and clothed by members of the committee out of
the funds of a weekly 'poor collection'. Any of the poor who were
subsequently found begging were to have their relief withdrawn
immediately. Church of Ireland congregations in Lurgan,
Magheralin and Ballinderry contributed an average of about £10
per year in the 1830s.[2] This money was then used to provide
food, clothing and coffins for the poor, as well as financing those

who agreed to care for orphaned and abandoned children. The Methodist Church at Thomas Street, Portadown, was also involved in such activities.

Outside the sphere of Churches, help was rare, although in large towns some societies existed to aid those in need. George Greer, a local businessman, told of one such group in Lurgan:

> We have a subscription in the town – a Philanthropic Society – where we distribute about 6*l.* a week to the people who beg on the streets. The inhabitants subscribe a certain sum per year, which is then distributed to the poor.[3]

Health-care provision was equally as limited, and with the county infirmary being in Armagh city, this locality was served by dispensaries in Lurgan, Portadown and Seagoe. These were funded by the Grand Jury of the county, with the following amounts being distributed in 1837: Lurgan – £57-15s; Portadown – £30-0s; Seagoe – £40-6s.[4]

In the early decades of the nineteenth century, the interest of the government was restricted to the appointment of Select Committees in 1819, 1823 and 1829, to examine the question of relief of poverty. Indeed, between 1825 and 1837, seven Poor Law Bills for Ireland were introduced to the British House of Commons, by private members – each one proving unsuccessful. However, the pressure for reform eventually told, and in 1833 the government established a Royal Commission to enquire into the conditions of the poorer classes in Ireland. The Commissioners, under the direction of Anglican Archbishop, Richard Whately, worked for three years in the most extensive survey of poverty ever undertaken in either Ireland or Britain. Their report, published in 1836, painted a very bleak picture of Irish society. One of the most significant findings was outlined as follows:

> We cannot estimate the number of persons in Ireland out of work and in distress during thirty weeks of the year at less than 585,000, nor the number of persons dependent upon them at less than 1,800,000, making the whole 2,385,000.[5]

This latter figure amounted to slightly less than one-third (30.7 per cent) of the total population, which at that time was estimated to be 7,764,411. The huge numbers living in abject poverty, meant that private charity was incapable of meeting their needs, the Commissioners argued. They stated that, in their opinion, state intervention, organised and run by central government, was essential. However, they hesitated to advocate a system modelled on the newly-amended Poor Law in England. The 1834 Poor Law Act for England provided poor relief only on condition that people entered a workhouse – there was to be no 'outdoor' relief. As they had discovered, Ireland, unlike England, had no large industrial workforce. Indeed, only 7.8 per cent of the population lived in towns with a population of 10,000 or more; in England this figure was 44 per cent.[6] Hence Ireland had large numbers of agricultural labourers, many landless, who were only employed during harvest time. Outside of this they were generally without work and unable to support their families, not through an unwillingness to work, but as a result of the environment in which they lived. Consequently, the Commissioners recommended that the government should introduce a number of schemes to promote the economic development of the country, with, for example, grants to aid reclamation of large areas of bogland and the development of fisheries. They also suggested that large-scale emigration to the British colonies would help reduce the burgeoning population. Such recommendations did not meet with the approval of a government dedicated to the economic doctrine known as laissez-faire, which in effect meant that there should be no interference by the government in the everyday running of the market. Perhaps not surprisingly, therefore, in September 1836, a new enquiry was commissioned, headed this time by the Chief English Poor Law Inspector, George Nicholls. He was requested to go to Ireland and judge the accuracy of the original investigation. He was also asked to indicate whether or not, in his opinion, a workhouse system would prove adequate to meet the Irish situation. However, Whately, for one, had no doubt as to the outcome of Nicholls' visit:

> He is gone on a tour through Ireland to form the conclusion that workhouses on a similar plan to those of England will be a safe and effectual remedy for the distress of Ireland: he will

come back with the conclusion, because he took it out with him, and he is not likely to lose it on the way.[7]

Whately's cynicism was well-founded as, after less than nine weeks in Ireland, Nicholls reported as the government hoped he would, recommending an extension of the workhouse system in Ireland. However, the 'Bill for the more effective relief of the Destitute poor in Ireland' had to pass through a number of stages in the Houses of Parliament. In the hiatus which followed, it was met with vociferous opposition by those most likely to be affected by it – the landowning class in Ireland.

The Bill provided relief for the poor based upon a compulsory rate determined by the amount of land owned. In his evidence to the Select Committee of 1830, George Greer had surmised that local areas would not be willing to undertake such compulsory assessment – by 1838 his thoughts had been vindicated. Local newspapers carried letters and editorials castigating in the strongest terms those who had framed the Bill. The *Newry Telegraph* declared the measure to be a bad one 'concocted by theorists who knew little or nothing of the people for whom they propose to legislate'. In a personal attack on Nicholls they stated that the Bill was 'founded upon an absurd and ridiculous report drawn up by an ignorant theorist.'[8] These sentiments were echoed in the many public meetings and subsequent petitions to Parliament from various localities, although couched in somewhat less direct terms. At a meeting held in the News Room in Portadown in March 1838, attended by 'numerous and respectable' inhabitants of the town, the following resolution was agreed upon to be presented in Parliament:

> Your Petitioners view with much alarm the provisions of the Irish Poor Law, now in progress through Parliament. That considering the hasty and ill-digested Report, upon which it is professedly based, we can only regard it as a very rash experiment, and as such we protest against the great outlay of money with which it is proposed to be accompanied. We would strongly, but respectfully, urge upon your Lordships, the rejection of the proposed measure altogether, and the adoption in its stead of an act empowering parishes in vestry to assess themselves, as they may see fit for charitable purposes. Should your Lordships, however, feel it expedient to pass into a law,

the measure at present contemplated... we earnestly entreat
that your Lordships will embody in it a clause limiting relief to
the sick, the impotent, the aged and also a clause of settlement.[9]

Similar sentiments were expressed in a petition from Tullylish
where it was felt that the Bill was 'dangerous and in the highest
degree objectionable', in that it proposed to transfer power from
local control to a Board 'unconnected with districts by property
or otherwise'.[10] In a resolution that was later to prove prophetic,
the Grand Jury of the county opined that the collection of any
rate imposed would prove 'most difficult' and in some districts
'perhaps impossible'.[11]

The essence of the opposition was the belief that the new system
would prove expensive to operate and become a burden on rate
payers. It was felt that care for the poor should be left to those
who lived in each locality, organising a voluntary subscription
society, akin to church donations, but on a more widespread
basis. Aside from the financial implications of the measure, many
feared that any system of relieving the poor would only serve to
perpetuate poverty and increase dependence on the state. George
Greer had alluded to this viewpoint when commenting:

I think if the labouring poor of Ireland were to be provided for,
they would not exert themselves to look for employment.[12]

However, as we shall see in later chapters, petitions and
resolutions could not dissuade the government from its chosen
path and the Bill was passed on April 30, becoming law two
months later on July 1, 1838.

Implementation of the Poor Law necessitated a division of the
country into administrative units known as Unions – 130 in total.
Each Union consisted of a group of electoral divisions, which, in
turn, were made up of a number of townlands. In accordance
with the governmental belief in making the Poor Rate as local a
charge as possible, the electoral divisions were made the unit
area of taxation, by means of rates levied on property owners in
relation to the value of their holdings. One of the inevitable
consequences of this policy was a fall-off in voluntary church
contributions, as people were unwilling to pay twice to aid the
poor. Hence, at the 1841 Easter Vestry of the Church of Ireland

in Moira, it was resolved that 'in consequence of the opening of the poorhouse, the collecting of alms for the poor in the church be suspended.' Similarly, the contributions from Donaghcloney Presbyterian Church declined from almost £11 in 1831 to £3 in 1847.[13]

Each Union was to have its own workhouse centrally situated to a market town, and administered by a Board of Poor Law Guardians who consisted of those elected by the rate-payers, together with ex-officio local men (no women were involved).

The Irish system was supervised by the full-time Board of Poor Law Commissioners in London who already supervised the English system. They, in turn, appointed a number of full-time Assistant Commissioners, each responsible for a number of Unions in adjoining counties. The workhouse was to be the embodiment of the Irish Poor Law and the attitude of those in power was reflected in the following statement by Nicholls, who now became the Resident Commissioner for Ireland:

> I wish to see the poorhouse looked to with dread by our labouring classes and the reproach for being an inmate of it extend downwards from father to son ... Let the poor see and feel that their parish, although it will not allow them to perish through absolute want, is yet the hardest task-master, the closest pay-master and the most harsh and unkind friend they can apply to.[14]

Thus the workhouses were to be an accurate reflection of this Dickensian ethos – not only were they offered as the sole medium for the provision of relief, they were also expected to provide a 'test' for that relief, being administered in such a fashion as to deter all but the truly destitute from applying.

Not surprisingly then, the architect who designed the buildings, George Wilkinson, was directed to make them uniform, cheap, durable and unattractive. The cost of each was to be only two-thirds that of similar English workhouses, with the Poor Law Commissioners commenting as follows:

> The style of building is intended to be of the cheapest description compatible with durability and simplicity of arrangement, all mere decoration being studiously excluded.[15]

Figure 1: Plan of 800 person workhouse.

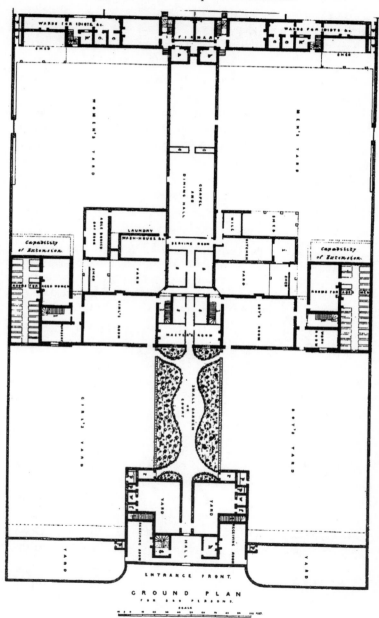

Wilkinson developed two basic workhouse plans: one to accommodate 400 people, the other 800, with both capable of expansion to include an extra 200.

The buildings met the demands of the Commissioners in that they were modest in the extreme – on the inside, the rough stone walls were not even plastered, but white-washed, while there were no ceilings, just bare rafters.

Further expense was spared as a result of two innovations initiated by Wilkinson. Firstly, the floors were made of mortar rather than boards or flagstones. Secondly, in place of bedsteads, he introduced sleeping platforms which were simply continuous raised wooden floors on either side of the dormitories or wards, where the inmates slept on straw mattresses.

The unpalatable nature of such institutions was further stressed by the Commissioners in their report for 1839-40:

> We are satisfied that the diet, clothing, bedding and other merely physical comforts may, in the workhouse, be better than in the neighbouring cottages and yet that none but the really destitute poor will seek for admission into the workhouse, provided that order and discipline be strictly maintained therein.[16]

Hence, life within the workhouse was to reflect the deterrent aspect of the buildings themselves. The regime was to be based on principles of order, discipline and regimentation strictly enforced by the master, the official responsible under the Guardians for the daily management of the house.

When they entered the building, paupers were immediately segregated according to sex, age and physical condition and then sent to different wards, each with their own yard for work. Consequently, families were broken up, wives separated from husbands, parents from children, sisters from brothers – they were only allowed to meet again at times appointed by the Guardians, usually a short period once a week. Furthermore, all paupers had to wear distinctive workhouse clothes and obey prison-like rules and regulations: boys could be flogged and adults put in the lock-up if they disobeyed.

The workhouse diet was monotonous and frugal in the extreme, with the Commissioners recommending:

> The workhouse diet must on no account be superior or even
> equal to the ordinary mode of subsistence of the labouring
> classes of the neighbourhood.[17]

This grim dogma, apparently inherent in all aspects of Poor
Law procedure, also applied to employment for inmates within
the workhouse, with the Commissioners remarking as follows:

> For every class of inmate, employment should be provided;
> but for the able-bodied it should be of such a nature as to be
> irksome and to awaken or increase a dislike to remain in the
> workhouse.[18]

In the light of such harsh regulations and Nicholls' avowed
hope that the poor would find the workhouse a 'most harsh and
unkind friend', it is perhaps surprising that anyone would wish to
enter such an institution. However this view fails to account for
the immense poverty then widespread in Ireland. Lurgan Union
bore a resemblance to many other parts of the country in that a
proportion of its population lived in primitive conditions and
some were prepared to sacrifice the relative freedom of their
cabins for the security of food and a bed in the workhouse,
regardless of the subsequent restrictions placed on their person.

Footnotes

1. Col. William Blacker's Diary, *The Blacker Day Book*, vol. v, p. 243
   Blacker Day Books.
2. Vestry Books of the Church of Ireland parishes in Drumcree,
   Lurgan, Magheralin Ballinderry and Portadown Methodist Church.
3. Minutes of evidence taken before the Select Committee on the
   State of the Poor in Ireland, 1830; evidence of George Greer, p.
   356.
4. *Ibid.* Appendices II and III.
5. M. Farrell, *The Poor Law and the Workhouse in Belfast, 1838-1948*,
   Public Record Office of Northern Ireland, 1978, p. 1.
6. B.J. Graham and L.J. Proudfoot (eds), *An Historical Geography of
   Ireland*, Academic Press, 1993, p. 161.
7. P. Durnin, *Derry and the Poor Law: a History of the Derry Workhouse*,
   The Waterside Community Local History Group, 1991, p. 35.
8. *Newry Telegraph*, 29 March, 1838.

9. *Ibid.*
10. *Ibid.* 24 April, 1838.
11. *Ibid.* 22 March, 1838.
12. Minutes of evidence taken before the Select Committee on the State of the Poor; evidence of George Greer, p. 356.
13. Vestry Books of Moira Church of Ireland and Donaghcloney Presbyterian Church.
14. M. Farrell, *The Poor Law*, p. 4.
15. C. Kinealy, *This Great Calamity: the Irish Famine 1845-1852*, Gill and Macmillan, 1994, p. 25.
16. M. Farrell, *The Poor Law*, p. 38.
17. *Ibid.* p. 5.
18. *Ibid.*

2.

Lurgan Union before the Famine

As we have seen, one of the stipulations of the new Poor Law was that each Union was to be centred around a market-town accessible to an area within a seven or eight mile radius. In County Armagh two such towns were deemed as meeting these requirements: the primatial city of Armagh was chosen as the centre of a Union incorporating the mid and southern parts of the county; the north of the county was centred around Lurgan. Other smaller areas of the county were distributed amongst the Unions of Banbridge, Newry, Dundalk and Castleblaney.[1] However, as Poor Law Unions did not acknowledge existing County boundaries, the new Lurgan Union also included parts of Counties Antrim and Down.

The Union, which was declared on 16 January 1839, contained, in 1841, a population of 71,128 on 79,201 acres. Such figures indicate that this area was densely populated. Indeed, two interconnected features of the Lurgan Union were predominant in this era – the linen industry and population density.

In 1840 nine Lurgan men were listed as linen and yarn merchants and one source has described the town as:

> a centre of fine linen and cloth production destined for the great houses and institutions of the world.[2]

The *Parliamentary Gazetteer of Ireland* (1846) stated that the linen and muslin manufacture was so extensively carried on in both town and country that the greater portion of the population was either fully or partially employed in it.[3] Local knowledge also reinforced this point with Colonel Blacker, in his submission to the Devon Commission, describing the areas thus:

> This is a manufacturing county and there are vast numbers of small farms... that are held by men who cultivate them and weave also.[4]

Because weaving enabled much of the population to gain a living largely independent of agriculture, many people married early and occupied very small farms. As soon as a son married he built a room onto his father's house and then gained some of the adjoining land. Consequently, John Hancock, agent to Charles Brownlow, felt justified in making the following observation:

> The linen manufacture thus offers the strongest inducement to subdivision, because a very small portion of ground, in additon to looms, will support a family.[5]

In this way, the Lurgan Union became 'one of the most populous districts in Ireland',[6] as Table 1 illustrates. Thus in this Union the average acreage per head of population was 1.1 acres and this is probably why Hancock asserted that some land was subdivided to such an extent as to be almost impossible to plough.[7] Table 2 shows that just under one half of all land holders had two acres or less.

In 1821 the population of the town was 2,715; by 1841 this had increased to 4,677. Although linen manufacture accounted for much of such population growth, it was not the sole reason.

It can be argued that the development of the linen industry in Lurgan ensured that the town was seen as a place of promise for migrants from the surrounding countryside. Thus, attracted by the prospect of work, many rural people found employment and acceptable living conditions in the town. In the period 1832-5 tradesmen were attracted by the building of Brownlow House, home of the local landlord. Indeed, as late as 1844, this construction was providing work for painters, masons, gardeners and general labourers.[8] However, it is interesting to note that, at a trades' conference in Dublin in 1837, complaints were made of how Scottish masons were being employed in preference to local tradesmen. The fact that the architect, Playfair, was Scottish, may have ensured that he preferred to work with men he knew, regardless of the consequences for local employment.[9]

Table 1: Population and Acreage

Electoral Division	Area (acres)	Population
CO. ARMAGH		
Breagh	3,666	3,196
Brownlowsderry	2,788	3,034
Carrowbrack	2,747	2,747
Cornakinnegar	2,189	1,830
Drumcree	4,724	3,865
Kernan	4,199	5,130
Lurgan	2,998	6,987
Montiaghs	5,848	3,480
Portadown	4,979	7,160
Tartaraghan	5,594	4,513
CO. DOWN		
Ballyleny	3,891	1,970
Cornakinnegar	1,514	917
Donaghcloney	3,026	1,277
Magheralin	3,918	2,969
Moira	6,097	4,154
Tullylish	4,734	5,217
Waringstown	4,101	4,548
CO. ANTRIM		
Aghagallon	5,469	3,862
Aghalee	2,499	1,450
Ballinderry	4,120	1,922
TOTAL:	79,201	71,128

Source: Agricultural Returns for the Year 1847, HC Papers, 1847-8 LVII (923), p. 58.

Further migration was encouraged by the development of the railway through Lurgan in the early 1840s and the subsequent road and footpath building. Attempting to quantify such migratory trends is difficult, but some pointers are available.

In the 1841 Census, 28 percent of the population of Lurgan was described as being principally involved in agriculture. This figure only makes sense when it is taken to be a definite indication of the recent arrival in the town of a considerable number of rural migrants. Otherwise, as McCorry suggests, the inference is that over 1,000 people were mainly involved in agriculture in an eighty-two acre town.[10]

Table 2: Land Ownership in Lurgan Union

Acres	No. of Owners
0 – 1	3,806
1 – 2	901
2 – 3	765
3 – 4	720
4 – 5	702
5 – 6	556
6 – 7	498
7 – 8	378
8 – 9	312
9 – 10	246
10 – 20	1,267
20 – 50	575
50 – 100	26
200 – 500	5
2,000 – 3,000	1

Source: The Devon Commission, 1844

The most likely explanation for this figure is that farmers, on moving to town, still referred to themselves as such and thus gave a totally disproportionate and distorted figure for this occupational area. Much evidence of such migration is provided by local church registers which record the baptisms of people from Magheralin, Seagoe and Derrymacash.[11]

Connell has asserted that while towns offered the prospect of employment, they also offered safety in numbers and a place to beg or sell rags.[12] Lurgan seems to have differed little in this respect. During this period of pre-Famine population increase the town attracted, along with those seeking employment, quite a high proportion of poorer migrants surviving at the lowest subsistence level.

Evidence of this was offered by Blacker who noted that the poor-rate in Lurgan was fifteen pence in the pound, in contrast to his own district near Portadown where the rate stood at five pence in the pound.[13]

However, it appeared that the town was able to cope with this influx of rural poor. Cellars, yards and tenements were supplemented by rows of houses of similar standard, while many of the least desirable town-courts came into being during this time. The standard of living experienced by those occupying such buildings may be gauged from a report authorised by the Lurgan Town Commissioners in 1856. Two doctors – Shaw and Gilbert – reported on what they termed 'a great want of ventilation, cleanliness, drainage etc., especially in and around the dwellings of the poor'. They commented further on the large numbers of people congregated in 'confined and wretchedly accommodated houses'. An example was cited of a lodging house at the Pound River which not only contained men and women, but also a pig and donkey – separate dwellings being recommended for the latter. The doctors lamented both the lack of privies and the filthy state of those already in use. They also advised the removal of slaughter houses, pig-houses and dung heaps to a safe distance from dwellings 'as such nuisances would tend to the spread of disease'. They concluded thus:

> In all the foregoing cases, we consider the premises to be in such a filthy and unwholesome condition that the health of the inmates and neighbours is thereby endangered.[14]

If rural migrants were prepared to live in virtual slum conditions such as these in town, we must enquire as to their standard of living prior to migration.

Fortunately we are given an in-depth insight into the condition of the labouring class by scrutinising the 1836 Report into the Conditions of the Poorer Classes – the outcome of which was supposed to have formed the basis for the Irish Poor Law.

This report graphically illustrates the low level at which many rural labourers lived. It also explains why they saw a move to the nearest town as offering an improvement in their standard of living.

Figure 2: Rare photograph of male labourer c. 1850s

Labourers' houses were typically very basic one-roomed mud cabins, occasionally built of stone and lime. They were described as 'wretched abodes', rarely approaching anything akin to comfort; and the same description applied to furniture which was in all essentials basic. More often than not there was only one bed in each house with most family members sleeping on straw bedding. Other items usually included a table, some stools and maybe a few shelves.[15] John Hancock estimated that approximately 30 percent of the local population lived in such circumstances,[16] and their clothing, which ranged from 'tolerably good' to 'wretched beyond description', was just as frugal.[17]

Indeed, this aspect of life proved annoying to a local clergyman:

> The clothing is, generally speaking, very bad... and the poverty of their attire is made an universal excuse for neglect of public worship.[18]

Labourers were generally employed for three to four days per week during the harvest months from March to June and August to November. Their wages averaged about one shilling per day without diet and between 6d and 8d with diet – giving an average annual wage of £10 to £15, depending on circumstances.

When unemployed, they either relied on the charity of others or resorted to begging, with one observer remarking:

> In such cases mendicancy is not infrequently the habitual trade of the children and sometimes of the wife too.[19]

Indeed, Colonel Blacker informed the Devon Commission that children could actually make money by collecting horse dung from the main roads.[20]

Given the general standard of living of this class, it is hardly surprising that the labourers' diet was monotonous in the extreme – consisting almost entirely of potatoes, meal and milk. Occasionally there were additions of salted herrings, oatbread and 'stirabout' (oatmeal and water). The inclusion of meat, however, was virtually unheard of. It would appear that the Rev. Ivers of Tartaraghan was stating the rule rather than the exception when he commented:

> Sometimes their breakfast, dinner and supper consist of potatoes.[21]

Such, then, was the standard of living enjoyed by the labouring class in Lurgan Union on the eve of the Famine and thus, it is not surprising that a move to a local market town would have been seen as a chance to enhance their lifestyle. For many, however, this remained an unobtainable dream and they ended up in the newly-constructed workhouse, placing their fate in the hands of the local Board of Guardians.

Footnotes

1. *Parliamentary Gazetteer of Ireland,* 1846, vol. ii, A. Fullerton & Co., 1846, p. 709.
2. F.X. McCorry, *Lurgan: An Irish Provincial Town,* 1610-1970, Inglewood Press, 1993, p. 69.
3. *Parliamentary Gazetteer,* 1846, vol. ii, p. 709
4. Evidence taken before the Commissioners appointed to Enquire into the Occupation of land in Ireland, 1844, The Devon Commission. Digest of Evidence, Part 1, H.C. 1845, (605), vol. xix, Evidence of Col Blacker, Q 11.
5. *Ibid.* John Hancock, Q. 55.
6. *Ibid.* Robert Dolling, Q. 5.
7. *Ibid.* John Hancock, Q. 55.
8. F.X. McCorry, *Lurgan,* p. 74.
9. *Dublin Evening Mail,* 28th December 1837.
10. F.X. McCorry, *Lurgan,* p. 71.
11. *Ibid.* p. 110.
12. P. Connell, *Changing Forces Shaping a 19th century Irish Town: a Case Study of Navan.* Occasional Papers no. 1, Maynooth 1978, pp 13-14.
13. Devon Commission, Col. Blacker, Q. 88.
14. Minute Book of Lurgan Town Commissioners, 27 November 1856, (P.R.O.N.I. LA51/2B/2).
15. First Report of Commissioners for Inquiring into the condition of the Poorer Classes in Ireland. Supplement to Appendix E, p. 285, H.C., 1836,vol. xxxii.
16. Devon Commission, John Hancock, Q. 5.
17. Poorer Classes Inquiry, Supplement to Appendix D, p. 336, H.C., 1836, vol. xxxi.
18. *Ibid.* Rev. C.K. Irwin, Drumcree, p. 285.
19. *Ibid.* pp. 275, 285, 334.
20. Devon Commission, Col. Blacker, Q. 9.
21. Poorer Classes Inquiry, Supplement to Appendix D, p. 285.

3.

The Lurgan Union Workhouse

The initial meeting of the newly-constituted Lurgan Union Board of Guardians took place at the Sessions House, Lurgan, on 1 March 1839. One of the first tasks of the new body was to establish the approximate number of destitute persons in the Union – each Guardian being required to forward the estimate in his locality. The total number amounted to 763, with over a quarter (200) resident in Lurgan and 50 in Portadown (see Table 3). This was further evidence of the fact that Lurgan had indeed attracted quite a large section of the rural poor to its environs.

Having established the level of destitution in the Union, the Guardians commenced the building of a workhouse to accommodate 800 persons. A six-acre site was chosen on the new road from Lurgan to Tandragee, in the townlands of Tannaghmore South and Aughnacloy (see Figures 3 and 4) and the building contract was awarded to the firm which had offered the lowest tender – Arthur Williams & Son of Dublin.

On completion of the building the Guardians advertised for a master and matron, stipulating that 'experience in the management of some public institution, and long and approved service in the army or navy is indispensable'. The eventual appointees, William and Sarah Thompson, were sent to the workhouse in the South Dublin Union to gain experience of managing such an institution.

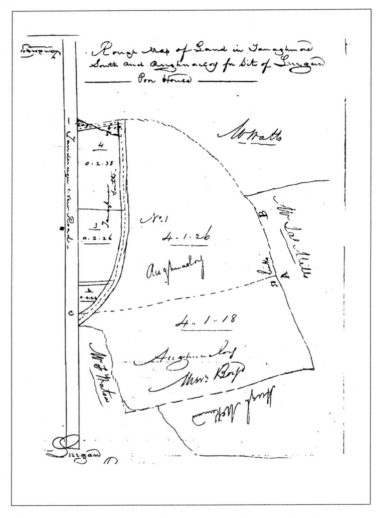

Figure 3: Sketch map of land chosen for Lurgan Workhouse

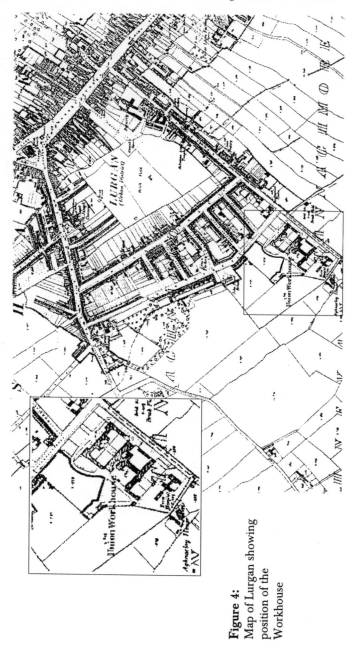

Figure 4:
Map of Lurgan showing
position of the
Workhouse

Shortly before the opening of the workhouse, the paupers' diet was determined as follows: breakfast – six ounces of meal and one third quart of buttermilk; dinner – three pounds of potatoes and one third quart of buttermilk; supper – six ounces of meal and one third quart of buttermilk. Children under seven years were to receive half of these quantities.[1]

Table 3: Estimated Number of Paupers in the Lurgan Union, March 1839

Aghagallon	20
Aghalee	12
Ballinderry	20
Ballyleny	24
Breagh	26
Brownlowsderry	16
Carrowbrack	10
Cornakinnegar	15
Donaghcloney	24
Drumcree	8
Kernan	84
Lurgan	200
Magheralin	57
Montiaghs	28
Moira	45
Portadown	50
Tartaraghan	30
Tullylish	35
Waringstown	59

On 22 February 1841, the workhouse was opened and received its first inmates – forty-three in total. The calibre of those seeking relief may be gauged from the following examples of people who entered in 1844:[2]

Sarah McCorry – thirty-four, spinner, widow, Catholic, Lurgan town, admitted with one child, both in fever; came to workhouse in a cart; dirty, filthy, ragged and miserable.

John Lavery – seventy-three, labourer, badly in fever, poor and naked; had a wife and five children outside, but they were very poor and not able to keep him.

Sarah Arnold – eighty-four, widow, Catholic, Waringstown, infection of lungs; wretched and filthy-looking; came in a cart.

William, Mary and Elizabeth Dynes – ten, seven and five respectively, Protestant; motherless and deserted by father – starved and nearly naked.

William King – sixty, flax dresser, Protestant, Lurgan town, rheumatic; came in a wheelbarrow; very wretched and dirty.

These cases illustrate a number of points concerning the Lurgan Union. Firstly, the workhouse catered for the most unfortunate members of society – the old and infirm, orphans, deserted children and mothers with young children. Secondly, and bolstering the findings of the 1836 Poor Enquiry, there existed a body of people living in extreme poverty and destitution in this area. Thirdly, a clue to the extent of reliance on the linen industry by the bulk of the population is given by references to 'spinner' and 'flax-dresser' in the list. Indeed, out of a total of 652 entrants to the workhouse in 1844, 172, or over one quarter, were listed as making their living from one branch or other of the linen industry.[3] Allowing for the old and infirm, this would appear to support the idea that even with a strong linen-base, many within this industry were surviving at the lowest subsistence level prior to the Famine.

Throughout the years 1841-5, the workhouse served its purpose in catering for the destitute without any great difficulty and numbers never rose above 55 percent of the capacity of the building. Table 4 shows the average weekly occupancy in the years leading up to the Famine.

Table 4: Average Workhouse Occupancy

YEAR	AVERAGE NO. PER WEEK IN WORKHOUSE
1841	283
1842	297
1843	258
1844	295
1845	222

Source: Lurgan Union Workhouse Admissions Register 1841-1845

However, in May 1845 the first break in the previously sound administration occurred when, after allegations of poor management and 'levity of conduct' were made against the master and matron, both resigned their positions.

The following months saw the appointment of two workhouse masters: Archibald Temple, who resigned after four months, and Charles Rooney (see Table 5). Such changes can hardly have proved conducive to effective management and indeed, the first evidence of inefficiency and carelessness was manifested in the doctor's report of October when he suggested that diahorrea and other connected problems among the young children were as a direct consequence of them being forced to sit in the nursery and schoolroom in cold, dank conditions.

Table 5: Lurgan Workhouse Masters 1840-47

NAME	APPOINTED	RESIGNED
William Thompson	11 Sept 1840	24 May 1845
Archibald Temple	28 June 1845	21 Oct 1845
Charles Rooney	22 Oct 1845	4 April 1846
John Meason	11 April 1846	6 Nov 1846 (Died)
James Easton	28 Nov 1846	13 April 1847
Charles Hinde	29 April 1847	1 May 1847
David Gillespie	1 May 1847	

Further to this, in February 1846 a visiting committee from the Poor Law Commissioners described the house as being in 'a very filthy and unclean state' and the Guardians ordered the house to be cleansed and washed every day – with any pauper who refused to work forfeiting breakfast.[4]

The first failure of the potato crop in August 1845 had a limited impact in the Lurgan Union. However, it did have important repercussions for the future. Between September and November sub-Inspector Little of the Portadown constabulary sent reports on the progress of the disease to Dublin. During this period it gradually emerged that approximately one-third of the crop had been damaged. The disease appeared to have been particularly virulent on wet heavy ground, whereas potatoes planted in light dry areas had not suffered to the same extent. Various attempts were made to save the 'sound' crop and the Rev. Henry Willis reported that the 'poor people' had endeavoured to store potatoes in pits, thus allowing air to pass through them and keep them dry. In numerous other cases diseased potatoes were sold cheaply for conversion into starch.[5]

Despite such manifestations of blight, Little stated 'several persons are of the opinion that the alarming reports are exaggerated'. Whether or not there was exaggeration, there can be little doubt that in an area where many depended on the potato, any loss would have been felt. John Woodhouse, in an attempt to ascertain the loss, gave the estimates for localities around Portadown shown in Table 6.

Table 6: Potato Crop Loss for Portadown, 1846

AREA	CROP LOST (%)
Drumcree	25
Breagh	33
Kernan	25
Portadown	25
Carrowbrack	25

Source: Woodhouse to Captain Kennedy, 4 April 1846, Relief Commission Papers.

Further evidence of a below-average crop is the fact that two months' supply of potatoes to the workhouse from Joseph Berry of Moira was found to be 'very insufficient, there being a great number of rotten and of very small size'.

As a consequence of this shortfall, potato prices rose sharply: in April 1845, they cost 1/11d per cwt.; in August 2/4d per cwt.; in December 3/- and by March 1846 they reached 3/3d per cwt. Indeed one supplier, Thomas Bullick, attempted to exploit the situation by demanding 4/- per cwt; however, the Guardians rejected this and he had to settle for 3/6d. The natural corollary of these price rises was the gradual reduction of potatoes in the workhouse diet, being replaced, at first, by bread and then by meal. Consequently in April, dinner consisted of 7 ozs of meal made into stirabout. Meal was convenient because it was a cheap substitute and in June the Guardians circulated tenders for supplies of the cheapest form available – yellow Indian cornmeal; this in spite of the fact that they declared themselves 'averse to an exclusively oatmeal diet'.

Figure 5: Invitation to Portadown Mont de Piétè

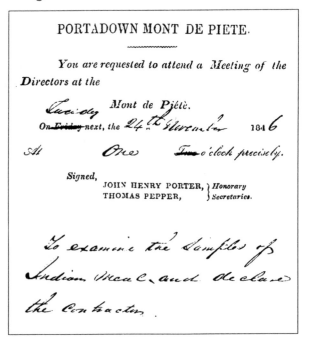

This shortage of potatoes was also evident in the general Union area. In Portadown, the Mont De Piétè Society had been established in 1838 as a loan fund in direct opposition to pawnbroker shops. However, it occasionally made money available for local charitable purposes and in May it made a grant of £50 towards the purchase of Indian meal for the poor of the area.[8]

However, the poor were turning in greater numbers to the workhouse and by June there were almost 450 inmates, with a quarter of these being in the fever hospital. This high proportion warranted a visit from Dr. Stevens of the Fever Commissioners with consequences that were to prove ominous for the future. In his report Stevens recommended that additional accommodation would be necessary in order to cope with increased numbers of fever patients. However, the Guardians rejected this recommendation and stated that,

> Dr. Bell turned out a great number of convalescents within these few days and consequently has much more room than when Dr. Stevens was here.[9]

Stevens also reported that fever was much more widespread than it should have been because Dr. Bell was allowing non-infected children to enter the fever hospital with their sick parents. In light of this the Commissioners concluded:

> Dr. Bell is unfit for his present office and we have therefore called an order to be prepared for his removal which we shall issue without delay unless he tenders his resignation.[10]

This appeared to be a reasonable demand given Bell's apparent negligence. However, the Guardians received it with 'concern and surprise' and in offering a vigorous defence of the medical officer they pronounced confidence in his 'skill, humanity… and great kindness of heart'.[11]

In fact, they went so far as to blame the Commissioners themselves for any problems which had arisen; the buildings, which had proved inadequate, had been constructed under guidelines set out by them whilst they had refused to supply paid nurses when the doctor had asked for them. Probably taken aback somewhat, the Commissioners acquiesced and on reviewing the evidence, exonerated Dr. Bell from two of four charges made against him. The Guardians were delighted with the outcome and shortly afterwards they unanimously resolved to increase Bell's salary by £20 per annum.[12] Their delight is understandable in that they had been vindicated in their stance and had offered resistance to interference from the central authorities.

Nonetheless, Dr. Bell had been found negligent on two points: he had turned out convalescent patients in order to reduce overcrowding, in effect leaving them to fend for themselves. At the same time he had actually contributed to the spread of fever by allowing healthy children to enter the hospital with their infected parents.

Considering the fact that workhouse numbers were rising, would such a man prove fit to hold the important office of medical officer? The next few months would show that the Guardians' 'success' was a hollow one, that their judgment was flawed and that Dr. Bell's services should have been dispensed with on receipt of the Commissioners' demand.

Footnotes

1. Lurgan Union Board of Guardians' Minute Book, 1839, p. 4.
2. Lurgan Union Board of Guardians' Admissions Register, 1844.
3. *Ibid.*
4. Lurgan Union Board of Guardians' Minute Book, 1841, p. 192.
5. Lurgan Union Board of Guardians' Admissions Register, 1844.
6. Lurgan Union Board of Guardians' Minute Books, 1841-5.
7. *Ibid.*
8. Minute Book of Portadown Mont de Piétè Society, 22 May, 1846.
9. Lurgan Union Board of Guardians' Minute Book, 1846, pp. 110-117.
10. *Ibid.* pp. 110, 137-40.
11. *Ibid.* pp. 137-40.
12. *Ibid.* pp. 137-40, 186-7, 249.

4.

Distress and Relief

Because of the partial failure of the potato crop in the 1845 season, there was a shortfall in the supply of seed potatoes for 1846.[1] Consequently it was reported that 'not so much has been planted on account of the high price and scarcity of seed' and the new crop was approximately ten per cent smaller than that of the previous year.[2] As a local constabulary report revealed:

> Many persons had decided on not planting potatoes to the same extent; but they have changed their minds, finding those planted to appear healthy and vigorous in their growth.[3]

Indeed in April, the Grand Jurors of the County reported 'favourably' on the state of the crop.[4]

Any such optimism about the new season proved to be ill-founded, however, as in July and August the blight struck again – this time with widespread and devastating effect. The *Northern Whig*, quoting from the Armagh Agricultural Report for August, gave the following account of the destruction:

> Mostly every potato field the eye could light on, had the appearance of having been blighted by frost, and in most instances, the petals of the blossoms of the late planted potatoes were observed to wither and shed, in the course of a few hours at times, by day and by night'.[5]

This report was corroborated by James Brown from Donaghcloney who informed the Lurgan Union Farming Society that on travelling from Warrenpoint to Lurgan, he could 'scarcely believe the smell along the road arising from the decomposition of the potatoes'.[6] Indeed, by the end of August it was reported from Portadown that at least half the crop was diseased. A member of the constabulary commented that out of thirty cartloads of potatoes examined at the local market, not one was free from disease.[7] The *Northern Whig* reported how Mr. Edgar from the town had forwarded some potatoes to the paper which had exhibited 'decided marks of the disease'.[8] Conclusive proof of the devastation was given in reply to a circular sent by the Commissioners. George Greer, on behalf of the Guardians, remarked that the blight had reappeared in every electoral division of the Union and had affected the entire crop.

Unlike 1845, the widespread failure had an immediate impact in the Union. From each area came harrowing reports of human suffering. In Derrymacash there was found to be 'an incredible amount of misery and disease' with the townland described as being in 'an awful state'. The Montiaghs brought the following report:

> It would be almost, if not utterly, impossible, in Ulster, to find a more wretched peasantry... whether as regards their lodging, clothing or food. They bear all the appearance of being steeped to the very lips in destitution and distress. Their hovels are frequently more like neglected pig-styes than human habitations.[9]

The poor of Drumcree were living in 'extreme deprivation and distress' whilst Derryhirk was said to vie in condition with the worst ever reported of Cahirciveen:

> The people are not fed, have little clothing and the huts are as miserable and as squalid-looking as the tenants.[10]

One local man was reported as saying,

> If there does not be an alteration soon, the creatures will have to rise and take the meal. Half of them is near mad with could (sic) and hunger, and what can they do?[11]

'Awful want and destitution on the part of those applying for relief' was witnessed in Donaghcloney, while Bleary seemed to suffer particularly badly:

> If there be those who have a morbid appetite for 'supping full
> of horrors' let them traverse Ballydougan, Clare, Loughans,
> Ballynabragget and Bleary and they will soon be satiated. I
> have found in lieu of independence, a broken spirit; instead of
> comparative prosperity, penury, starvation and death. The
> pestilence is abroad and its havoc is truly and absolutely fearful.[12]

In Moira comment was made on the 'destitute condition of the
labouring classes in consequence of the failure of the potato'.
One woman with a young child had not tasted food in days. She
had been deserted by her husband and 'thrown destitute and
starving upon the wide world'.[13]

Finally, from Portadown, there was reported to be 'great distress
prevailing amongst our very numerous class of working people',
with Lord Gosford declaring the population to be 'very dense
and in a most wretched state'.[14]

The Lurgan Union was not alone in its suffering, however, and
on 6 January 1847 the *Belfast Vindicator* carried the following
report:

> It is, unhappily, too evident that Ireland is now suffering under
> an awful calamity – famine, disease and premature death,
> prevailing in some degree everywhere. Accounts multiply of
> destitution and suffering and death in their most appalling forms;
> the cry of distress is becoming louder every day; the prospects
> for the future are very dark.[15]

With the workhouse full, 'the cry of distress' in this Union was
met by the establishment of local relief committees. Such groups
had emerged in other parts of the country in response to the
failure of 1845, but they had proved unnecessary here. However,
in the worsening conditions of the winter of 1846 voluntary relief
committees proved to be an essential component of attempts to
counteract the effects of food scarcity. They also illustrated how
the Poor Law, restricted to relief inside a workhouse, proved
totally ineffective when dealing with widespread local distress.

By December such committees had been established in Lurgan,
Portadown, Drumcree, Tartaraghan and Moira. In January further
groups emerged in Donaghcloney, Tullylish, Magheralin,
Ballinderry and Kernan (see Figure 6).[16]

Figure 6: Lurgan Poor Law Union 1847

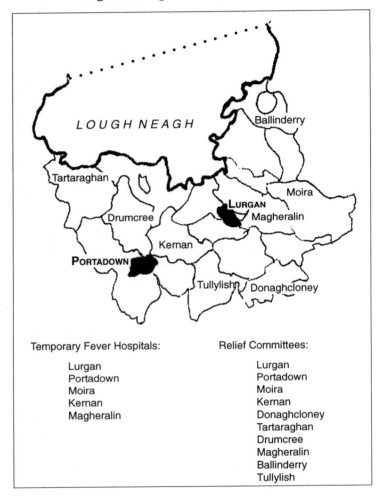

For the most part, the catalyst for establishing the relief committees was the local clergy, both Catholic and Protestant (jointly), with the local landed gentry either participating at a minor level or solely through subscription. The most important aspect of the committees was their ability to purchase and distribute food – mainly meal and soup. Finance was raised by

Figure 7: Subscribers to Lurgan Relief Fund

A List of Subscriptions collected and paid to the Treasurer of the Lurgan Relief Committee in the County of Armagh, in aid thereof

	£	s	d		£	s	d
Right Honourable Lord Lurgan	150	..	..	Amount Brought up	410	10	..
Boyd & Watts	20	..	..	Rev.d W. P. Bolton		5	..
Dean Waring	20	..	..	Rev.d Wm. O'Brien		5	..
James W. Murray	20	..	..	Robert Morris		5	..
George Greer	20	..	..	John Johnston		5	..
J & H. Cuppage	15	..	..	Arthur W. Forde		5	..
Joseph H. Boyd	10	..	..	John W. Greer		5	..
Samuel Watts	10	..	..	W & T. Greer		5	..
James Malcolm	10	..	..	Henry Greer (Woodville)	1	1	0
John Hazlett	10	..	..	John & Hu. Lockhart		5	..
John Hancock Jr.	10	..	..	Joseph Greer		5	..
Northern Bank	10	..	..	Mrs. Paul		3	..
Ulster Bank	10	..	..	Mrs. Todd		3	..
Belfast Bank	5	..	..	Mrs. Watson		3	..
Ruddell Todd	10	..	..	Mrs. Burke		3	..
James Boyd	10	..	..	Miss O'Donnell		3	..
Mrs. M. Boyd	10	..	..	Miss Greer		3	..
Thomas Hall	10	..	..	Mrs. Whittle		2	..
C & J. Hall	5	..	..	Abraham Bell		2	..
Doctor Bell	5	..	..	Miss Crawford		2	..
John Cuppage & Co.	5	..	..	Matthew Wells		2	..
Wm. Armstrong John	8	..	..	Thomas Stanley		2	..
Wm. Armstrong Jr.	3	..	..	J Mrs. Johnston		2	..
John Armstrong	2	10	..	John Hazelton		2	..
Rob.t Watson	5	..	..	Mrs. Gilbert		2	..
Mr. Stewart	5	..	..	Sam.l Greer		2	..
William Watson	2	..	..	Robert Stanley		2	..
Mr. Shiells of Liverpool	5	..	..	William Thompson		2	..
Doctor Hannay	5	..	..	Wm. B. Morris		2	..
				Rob.t Morrison	1	10	..
carried up	410	10	..	Carried forward	500	1	..

means of public subscription to a relief fund and any amount subscribed was supplemented by an equal amount from central government funds in Dublin. Most subscribers were either clergymen, gentry or farmers, although outside relief agencies did play an important part in augmenting local finance. Thus, we find the following agencies supporting relief in the Lurgan Union: the Belfast Relief Fund, the Central Relief Committee of the Society of Friends (see Appendix D), the National Club, London, the Ladies' Dublin Association, the Belfast Ladies' Association, the Durham Relief Association, the Irish Relief Association and the Calcutta Fund (see Figure 8).[17]

Such external aid was all the more important when we consider the fact that some landlords appeared indifferent to the suffering of their tenants. In letters to the local press, the Rev. Clements of Tartaraghan complained bitterly about the obduracy of local landlords:

> There are only two resident landed proprietors within the parish… The largest estate is under the administration of the Lord Chancellor for debt with no help whatsoever being obtained from it for its starving tenantry. A large portion of the parish is bog, the property of absent proprietors and upon it are located a large number of most wretched tenants who are not assisted by the landlord.[18]

Indifference on the part of some members of the landed class was compounded by red tape and bureaucracy which meant that delay was encountered by committees when applying for financial assistance. A possible explanation is that the Relief Commission Offices in Dublin were inundated with such requests. Nevertheless, on occasions, the chairmen of local committees had to send two or three letters informing the authorities of the amount subscribed locally and enquiring as to when government money would be forthcoming. For example, on 28 March, William Morris, local postmaster and treasurer of the Lurgan Relief Fund, sent a letter to Dublin stating that £53 had been subscribed and asking for an equivalent amount – by 17 April he had not received a reply.[19] Likewise in Ballinderry, the local treasurer, Alexander Miller, wrote to Dublin on 22 February; by the beginning of March he had heard nothing.[20]

Figure 8: Income and expenditure of Drumcree Relief Fund
up to 31 August 1847

Income	£	s	d
To amounts of private subscriptions viz:			
From the Parish Clergymen	35	0	0
From Landed Proprietors of the Parish	129	0	0
From Landholders of the Parish	71	2	0
From Inhabitants of Portadown	13	3	0
SUB-TOTAL	248	5	0
To Grants from Charitable Associations viz:			
From the Society of Friends	20	0	0
From the Central Relief Fund	30	0	0
From the Irish Relief Association	30	0	0
From the Belfast Relief Fund	15	0	0
From the British Association	50	0	0
SUB-TOTAL	145	0	0
From friends at a distance	22	0	0
Two donations from Lord Lieutenant	256	0	0
Transmitted by His Grace the Lord Primate	20	0	0
To Cash, received from Applicants for Relief, for 63 tons, 6cwt, 2qrs, 27lbs of Indian Corn Meal, sold at reduced price of 2s. per score	709	7	6
TOTAL	1,400	12	6

Expenditure	£	s	d
By cash paid for a boiler	2	3	0
By cash paid for 63 tons, 6cwt, 2qrs, 27lbs of Indian Corn Meal, retailed to Persons Relieved at a reduced price	1,069	1	0
By cash paid for 16 tons, 1cwt, 2qrs, 21lbs of Indian Corn Meal, gratuitously Distributed to Sick and Destitute	219	17	5
By cash paid for 25cwt of rice, given gratis to Poor by order of Committee of Irish Association, purchased with grant	30	0	0
By value of 8 bags of rice, from British Association, distributed gratis to Sick, Poor	16	0	0
By paid transport of meal and rice	2	3	0
By cash paid for Rice, distributed gratuitously	20	0	0
By paid account of Printing and Stationery	5	10	0
By paid sundry postages	1	12	1
By balance in Treasurers' hands	36	6	0
TOTAL	1,400	12	6

Source: Newry Telegraph, 9 October 1847.

Figure 9: The Rev. Canon David Babbington,
Curate of Drumcree 1838-48

Despite such problems, local relief committees did manage to fulfill their purpose of selling or distributing food. In Lurgan, the Church of Ireland Rector, the Rev. William Oulton, was selling 'good substantial nourishing broth' together with a piece of bread, at one penny per quart to 1,700 people. A separate relief committee under the auspices of the Primitive Wesleyan Methodists was aiding a further 35 families. The Drumcree Fund was giving 'weekly aid to 450 destitute families,[21] amounting to 2,300 people,' with the Rev. Babbington, the secretary, commenting:

> I am prepared to state there is not a single family upon our relief list able to live without charitable assistance – without this, many would have perished from want.[22]

In Ballinderry relief consisted of sales of Indian meal at half-price whilst in Donaghcloney, Kernan and Moira, soup was being distributed through local kitchens with the latter committee

Figure 10: The Rev. W.H. Wynne, Rector of Moira, 1836-73

supplying about 300 people, two-thirds of whom bought the soup at a halfpenny per quart, with the rest being dispensed gratuitously.[23]

In Portadown, Tullylish and Bleary the poor initially received meal twice weekly.[24] However with conditions worsening, upwards of 40 cwts of meal and 120 gallons of soup were being distributed each day, meal at 1d. per pound. Nearly one hundred families in the Shane's Hill-Ballydougan area were benefiting from such aid. The rector of Tullylish, the Rev. W.B. Yeats, grandfather of the famous literary figure, revealed that over 3,000 people were receiving meal rations and gave this sad depiction of those applying for relief:

> Six members of the committee are engaged every Tuesday and Saturday from ten in the morning until half past six in the late evening endeavouring to supply the poor people's wants; many a heart-rending and piteous claim we have to meet by clubbing a collection in the room to enable the applicant to purchase a few pounds of meal to bring home to a starving family; for our rules are so stringent as to prevent us from giving to any parties, but such is the distress of the people this rule must be relaxed.[25]

Figure 11: The Rev. W.B. Yeats, Rector of Tullylish, 1838-1861

One of the worst-affected areas was Tartaraghan where, as we have seen, the Rev. Clements castigated what he termed the 'evil effects of absenteeism'.[26] A soup kitchen and meal fund were established to cater for over 1,300 'destitute persons', a number which was 'expected daily to increase'.[27]

Figure 12: Steam boiler used in soup kitchens, made in Lisburn

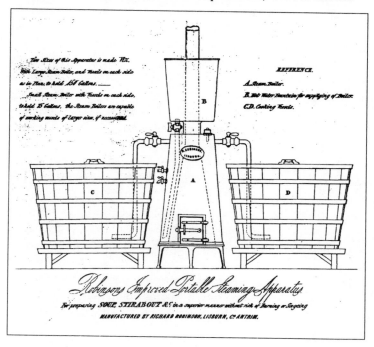

The following illustration of the level of distress in the locality was sent by Clements to the Commissioners in Dublin:

> Both weavers and labourers are daily becoming less equal to work and starvation is pictured in their countenances. Numbers are subsisting on less than one meal *per diem* and upon raw turnips and any herbs they can gather. Already one case of death from starvation has occurred... and several have only just been preserved from it, while fever has attacked very many in the district. Within the last few days, parties of twenty to thirty famishing men have been traversing the county demanding assistance. In the absence of all public works of any kind, and when our poor houses are nearly filled, we hardly know where to turn for assistance.[28]

Clements' reference to the lack of any public works scheme is significant in that it further highlighted the inability or unwillingness of local landlords to cater for their tenants. Such schemes were the preferred method of relief offered by a government determined to see that the poor should be put to work rather than offered charity. Often the work involved the construction of roads and paths which were not required. This is not surprising when it is understood that the government stipulated that such works could not be 'reproductive' and hence must not profit individuals or compete with capitalist entreprise. However in this area some landlords utilised the public works to fulfil their long-held desire to drain low-lying land around Lough Neagh. Many attempts had been made to carry out such drainage in the previous 20 years. Significantly, however, a government-sponsored drainage scheme in the early 1840s overlooked the demands of local landlords.

Not surprisingly, therefore, in October 1846, in response to 'the consequence of the calamity in question', Lord Lurgan advocated such drainage work as being 'the most desirable course to pursue... for the poorer class of tenantry and for those who are dependent on daily labour for their support'.[29] The Duke of Manchester also initiated such a scheme on his lands. The Board of Works sanctioned drainage work in the Union to the value of £23,000.

Nevertheless, some felt that the drainage relief work alone did not meet the needs of the people and in December a memorial was presented to Lord John Russell from concerned gentlemen in Portadown. In asking the government to encourage emigration and the cultivation of wastelands, they requested that the authorities convene an extraordinary Presentment Session in order to sanction relief works based on road, fence and bridge building.[30]

However, when Lord Lurgan became aware of such a request, he wrote to Dublin strongly advising against such a move and castigating those who sought it:

> The barony of O'Neilland West is proverbial for its multiplicity of roads and the extension of them would be unnecessary and injurious. I thrust therefore that when this is considered, together

Figure 13: Poster announcing a public meeting, 1846

TOWN OF PORTADOWN.

In pursuance of a Requisition which I have received, Signed by a majority of the Commissioners of this Town, I do hereby convene a

PUBLIC MEETING

of the Inhabitants, to be held at

The Public Room at the New Market,

On Monday, the 28th day of December, Inst., at the hour of 12 o'clock, noon,

For the purpose of considering what further Measures are necessary for the RELIEF OF THE POOR, and Providing for the present Distress, and also to make such APPLICATIONS TO GOVERNMENT, and adopt such PETITIONS TO PARLIAMENT, as the State of the Country may appear to require.

Dated this 22nd day of December, 1846.

JOHN OBINS WOODHOUSE,

Chairman, Town Commissioners.

EVANS, Printer, opposite Court House, Lurgan.

Figure 14: The Duke of Manchester's drainage scheme, 1846

TO THE

TENANTRY

ON THE

DUKE OF MANCHESTER'S ESTATES.

The DUKE OF MANCHESTER, anxious to alleviate the Distress which the failure in the Potato Crop is likely to occasion, has directed me to make such arrangements as will provide employment for the TENANTS and COTTIERS on his ESTATES, in the execution of Works which will be of permanent utility.

Having himself already opened the principal Water-courses on his property, the Drainage of the Land has been greatly facilitated, and His Grace now proposes to advance money, without Interest, to such Tenants as are anxious to improve their Farms by Thorough-draining, under the direction of the Agricultural Inspectors; the Sums so advanced to be repaid by TEN equal Yearly Instalments.

When it is borne in mind that Thorough-drainage, properly carried on, is found to repay the expense in Five Years by the increased value of the Crops, the extension of the time for repayment to Ten Years will be found more than sufficient. I beg to call the attention of the small Farmers to the necessity of preparing their Land immediately for the ensuing Crop; a quantity of SEED RYE shall be provided, at First Cost, to be repaid after the harvest of 1847; and to those who prepare Ground for PARSNIPS, a portion of SEED will be given, together with TURNIP SEED at the proper season, as hitherto, without any charge.

HENRY JOHN PORTER,
AGENT.

Tandragee Castle,
October 31, 1846.   James Henderson, Printer, Newry.

with the evils of draining the people off from their ordinary occupations, your excellency will not accede to a memorial of which I believe every proprietor in the barony is totally ignorant.[31]

There are a number of possible reasons as to why Lord Lurgan was so much in favour of the drainage work schemes. In comparison to other landlords in the area he appears to have been reasonably broad-minded. Hence it is likely that he did not wish to see his tenants employed in soul-destroying and pointless schemes involving stone-breaking and road-building. Indeed the county surveyor, in a report to the Grand Jury, commented that those involved in drainage schemes appeared much happier than their counterparts on the roads.

Figure 15: Lord Lurgan's drainage scheme

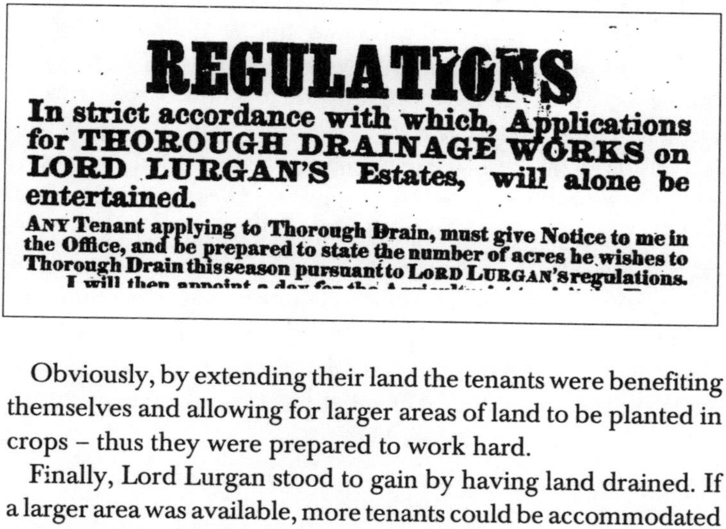

REGULATIONS

In strict accordance with which, Applications for **THOROUGH DRAINAGE WORKS** on **LORD LURGAN'S** Estates, will alone be entertained.

ANY Tenant applying to Thorough Drain, must give Notice to me in the Office, and be prepared to state the number of acres he wishes to Thorough Drain this season pursuant to LORD LURGAN'S regulations.

I will then appoint a day for the

Obviously, by extending their land the tenants were benefiting themselves and allowing for larger areas of land to be planted in crops – thus they were prepared to work hard.

Finally, Lord Lurgan stood to gain by having land drained. If a larger area was available, more tenants could be accommodated and thus rental income would be increased. Therefore, in Lord Lurgan's estimation, drainage benefited all those involved, both in the short and the long-term, alleviating distress by providing a larger landed area.

Consequently only a relatively small proportion of relief work in the Lurgan Union resembled that undertaken in most other areas. The following hills were lowered: Piper's Hill, Webb's Hill, Geddis' Hill, Furfey's Hill, Bunton's Hill, Cargan Hill and High Moss Hill. Hollows were filled in, in the townlands of Cornakinnegar, Killaughey, Silverwood, Turmoyra, Drumnakerin, Doneygreagh, Clankillvoragh, Derrytagh, Derryadd, Ballynay, Cloncore and Annagh. Repairs were also carried out on the mail-coach road between Lurgan and Whitehall and the road from Portadown to Tandragee.[32]

Nevertheless, the determination of Lord Lurgan was not shared by many of the landed class and the letter from Portadown reflects concern that not enough was being done to assist those in distress. Hence, it is not surprising to find that, in such areas, desperate people resorted to desperate measures.

On 13 January 1847, the police in Portadown reported that 'men to the number of five and twenty or thirty armed with flintlocks' stole fifty bags of flour from a barge at Maddin's Bridge.[33] In the following weeks similar attacks were made on boats belonging to the Ulster Canal Company in which barrels of flour and Indian meal were taken.[34] It is worth pointing out, however, that although these boats contained large and varied cargoes, it was only food that was stolen – thus emphasising the fact that such acts were not those of petty thieves, but of people prepared to go to any lengths to obtain food.

At a subsequent meeting of the county magistrates, outrage was expressed at such developments, with the gentlemen believing the police to be 'totally inadequate in point of numbers to take the duty-keeping watch'.[35] In order to prevent a recurrence of such actions they recommended that,

> a portion of Her Majesty's regular troops might be advantageously employed in this service as well as in protecting the boats laden with provisions on the Newry Canal.[36]

However, the vast majority of people remained within the boundaries of the law and for many the only assistance available was at the local workhouse. In this institution though, daily tragedy was becoming commonplace.

Footnotes

1. Constabulary Reports 1846, Cos. Armagh, Down and Antrim.
2. *Ibid.* Tullylish 30 May 1846.
3. *Ibid.* Magheralin/Moira 30 May 1846.
4. Lord Gosford to the Lord Lieutenant, 24 April 1846, Relief Commission Papers.
5. *Northern Whig*, 8 September 1846.
6. *Ibid.* 3 September 1846.
7. Sub-Inspector Little to Lord Lieutenant, 24 August 1846, Relief Commission Papers.
8. *Northern Whig*, 24 June 1846.
9. *Banner of Ulster*, 16 February, 1847.
10. *Ibid.* 12 February, 1847.
11. *Ibid.*
12. *Ibid.*
13. *Ibid.* 2 March, 1847.
14. Woodhouse to Dublin Castle, 12 December, 1846, Relief Commission Papers.
15. *Belfast Vindicator*, 6 January 1847.
16. Relief Commission Papers, Reports from throughout the Union, 1846-7.
17. *Ibid.* Reports from Relief Committees in Cos. Armagh, Antrim and Down, 1847.
18. *Ibid.* Rev. Clements to R.J. Routh, 1 January 1847.
19. *Ibid.* W. Morris to W. Stanley, 14 April 1847.
20. *Ibid.* Alexander Miller to R.J. Routh, 27 February 1847.
21. *Ibid.* Rev. Oulton to W. Stanley, 4 February 1847.
22. *Ibid.* D. Babbington to R.J. Routh, 3 February 1847.
23. *Ibid.* Henry Wynne to R.J. Routh, 5 February 1847.
24. W.B. Yeats to Lord Lieutenant, 21 January, 1847.
25. *Ibid.*
26. Rev. Francis Clements to R.J. Routh, 1 January 1847.
27. *Ibid.* Clements to R.J. Routh, January 1847.
28. *Ibid.* Clements to R.J. Routh, January 1847.
29. Lord Lurgan to Lord Lieutenant, 5 January, 1847, Distress Papers.
30. Memorial of Portadown residents to Lord John Russell, 28 December, 1846, Distress Papers.
31. Lord Lurgan to Lord Lieutenant, 5 January, 1847, Distress Papers.

32. County Armagh Grand Jury Books, Arm 4/1/61, P.R.O.N.I., pp. 153-203.
33. Portadown Constabulary Report, 13 January 1847, Outrage Papers.
34. *Ibid.* Portadown, 23 January 1847.
35. *Ibid.* Tandragee, 23 February 1847.
36. *Ibid.*

5.

The Workhouse in Crisis

The most noticeable manifestation of the failure of the potato crop was the increase in the number of people entering the workhouse. At the end of September 1846, the number was 313; by October this reached 432; by November, 598 and by the end of December the workhouse was full to capacity with 805 inmates.

This increase in admission rates was accompanied by a corresponding rise in the number of deaths. Throughout the year the average number of deaths per month was about 14 but in November, 31 paupers died and in December, 58 deaths occurred.[1]

In the first week of January there were 18 deaths recorded; in the second week the number was 36, and for the week ending 16 January the total reached 55 deaths.[2] The pages of the visiting chaplains' notebooks previously occupied with details of 'divine services' and 'scripture readings' now told a sorry tale of multiple burials, with both the Catholic and Episcopalian chaplains performing interments on a daily basis.[3]

Concern was expressed by the Commissioners in Dublin and on 16 January they sent a letter to the Guardians indicating their regret at what they termed the 'great mortality' in the workhouse and requiring a detailed report from Dr. Bell on the reasons for the high number of deaths. Perhaps mindful of the report of Dr. Stevens in May 1846, they also asked for a report on the sanitary conditions in the building.

In his communication Bell stated that many deaths had occurred because numerous people had entered the workhouse in a sick condition and had died shortly afterwards. Thus,

> mortality in the workhouse is much greater than under ordinary circumstances and it is a well-known fact that many dying persons are sent for admission merely that coffins may be thereby obtained for them at the expense of the Union.[4]

In relation to sanitation, he reported that as there were four times the usual number of inmates, the building was now overcrowded and consequently it had been impossible to provide dry bedding:

> sleeping upon damp beds has increased fever and bowel complaints which have in many cases proved fatal.[5]

However, the doctor concluded his report with optimism by arguing that the cause of such deaths would be largely eradicated with the purchase of new bedding and the creation of a proper drying house.

Figure 16: Lurgan workhouse deaths per week,
January to March 1847

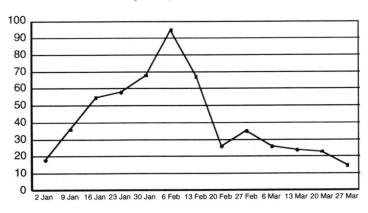

Such a statement, whether to placate the Commissioners or not, was soon shown to be rather utopian as in subsequent weeks mortality levels, far from falling, actually increased. In the week ending 23 January, 58 died; and the trend continued upwards;

30 January – 68 deaths; 6 February – 95; 13 February – 67 (see Figure 16).[6]

Given that large numbers were dying throughout the country, the Lurgan figures may be thought to be representative of the time. However, on examining the general mortality levels, this belief proves to be ill-founded. The numbers dying in the Lurgan workhouse in the first six weeks of 1847 represented the highest levels of such mortality in Ulster.

For example, in the week ending 6 February 1847, there were 95 deaths in the workhouse in Lurgan. This represented slightly less than one-fifth of the province's total mortality for that week – 529; the second highest was 30 deaths in Enniskillen workhouse. Nationally, the highest number was in Cork where, with a workhouse population of 5,338, 128 deaths had occurred. In the province of Connacht the highest level was in Loughrea workhouse in Co. Galway where, with 524 inmates, 26 had died.

Figure 17: Return of Paupers, Lurgan Union, week ending 6 February 1847

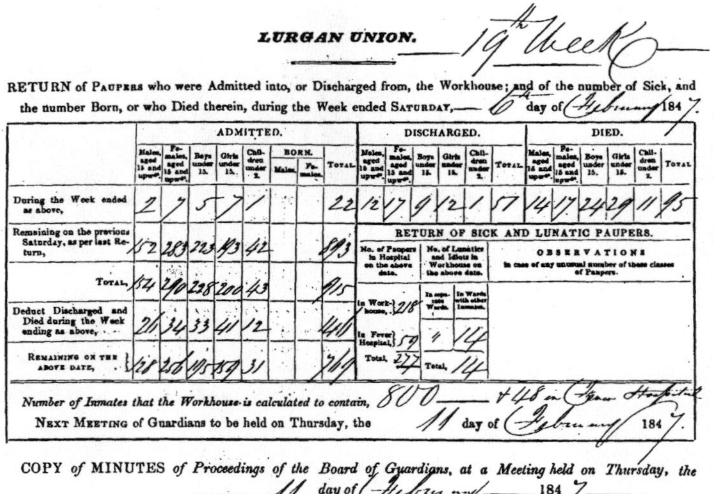

LURGAN UNION. 19th Week

RETURN of PAUPERS who were Admitted into, or Discharged from, the Workhouse; and of the number of Sick, and the number Born, or who Died therein, during the Week ended SATURDAY, 6th day of February 1847.

	ADMITTED. Males, aged 15 and upwds.	Females, aged 15 and upwds.	Boys under 15.	Girls under 15.	Children under 2.	BORN. Males.	BORN. Females.	TOTAL.	DISCHARGED. Males, aged 15 and upwds.	Females, aged 15 and upwds.	Boys under 15.	Girls under 15.	Children under 2.	TOTAL.	DIED. Males, aged 15 and upwds.	Females, aged 15 and upwds.	Boys under 15.	Girls under 15.	Children under 2.	TOTAL.
During the Week ended as above,	2	7	5	7	1			22	12	17	9	12	1	51	14	17	24	29	11	95
Remaining on the previous Saturday, as per last Return,	152	283	223	193	42			893												
TOTAL,	154	290	228	200	43			915												
Deduct Discharged and Died during the Week ending as above,	21	34	33	41	12			141												
REMAINING ON THE ABOVE DATE,	128	256	195	159	31			769												

RETURN OF SICK AND LUNATIC PAUPERS.

No. of Paupers in Hospital on the above date.		No. of Lunatics and Idiots in Workhouse on the above date. In separate Wards.	In Wards with other Inmates.	OBSERVATIONS in case of any unusual number of these classes of Paupers.
In Workhouse,	218			
In Fever Hospital,	59	4	14	
Total,	277	Total,	14	

Number of Inmates that the Workhouse is calculated to contain, 800 — + 48 in Fever Hospital

NEXT MEETING of Guardians to be held on Thursday, the 11 day of February 1847.

COPY *of* MINUTES *of Proceedings of the Board of Guardians, at a Meeting held on Thursday, the* 11 day of February 1847

PRESENT: *In the Chair,* Lord Lurgan

Lurgan's total of 67 deaths in the following week was second in Ulster behind that of Glenties, Co. Donegal, where, out of a total of 426 inmates, 69 had died. The highest figure was once again Cork where 164 paupers had died.[7] It is worth noting that Glenties was later to be deemed as one of the 'distressed districts' by the British Relief Association – the only one in Ulster; as such, large-scale relief was required to stave off widespread poverty and hunger. At the same time, Cork has become synonymous with the horrors of famine and the existence of mass famine graves. So, in the early months of 1847, the Lurgan area, described by a local paper as a 'prosperous and thriving town'[8] was suffering a level of workhouse mortality on a par with the worst-affected areas in the country. Figure 18 shows the workhouse deaths for each month in the two years 1846 and 1847.

Figure 18: Lurgan Workhouse Deaths per month, 1846 and 1847

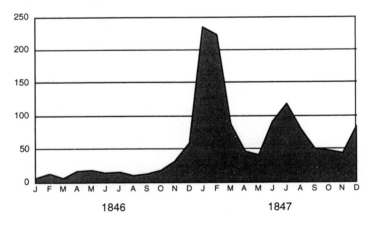

Dr. Bell's explanation that many deaths had occurred from sleeping on wet beds does not appear to have been entirely satisfactory as members of staff, presumably enjoying better accommodation than the paupers, began to fall ill. By late January the porter had dysentery and the assistant ward master, together with the schoolmaster, were ill in fever. In February the assistant ward master died and the clerk was suffering from the 'high symptoms of dysentery'.[9]

In a desperate attempt to alleviate what the Guardians called 'this dreadful visitation'[10] two remedies were attempted. Firstly, all available space was to be utilised in order to avoid overcrowding; thus the aged and infirm women were moved to a room above the stairs and the women's day room was acquired for hospital purposes. However, the Guardians felt that more drastic action was required and on 5 February they issued the following announcement:

> Notice is hereby given that in consequence of the present state of the workhouse and fever hospital, the Guardians have been obliged to close their doors for the present against all further admissions.[11]

As a consequence, admissions were restricted to a trickle throughout the period from February to April, with the authorities only allowing large numbers of applicants back in May.

A second measure taken by the Board was to request a visit by three 'eminent physicians' in order to remedy the 'unprecedented extension of disease and death'. The doctors – Thompson, Cumming and Purden – recommended that a third medical officer, along with Doctors Bell and McVeagh, was essential to meet the current epidemic. They also conveyed the opinion that the present paupers' diet was inadequate in that recently they had been receiving soup for dinner, and four ounces of rice for supper, instead of bread and buttermilk. The doctors considered such a diet to be insufficient to meet the needs of the paupers and recommended the following regime: breakfast – three and a half ounces of meal and porridge, and one quarter pint of buttermilk; dinner – six ounces of bread and one pint broth; supper – three ounces of bread and one quarter pint of buttermilk. They also stipulated that the porridge was to be made entirely of oatmeal, not Indian corn meal.[12]

The closure of the workhouse and visit of the doctors suggests that the authorities and medical staff were having severe problems coping with the numbers of destitute persons now prevailing in the Lurgan Union. Indeed in a communication to the Relief Commissioners' Office in Dublin, John Hancock reported that of 313 cases on the books of the Lurgan Dispensary, 136 were suffering from fever and dysentery; for the same period in 1846 this total was 20.[13]

The extent of the epidemic may be gauged by Hancock's enquiry as to whether the Central Board of Health could appoint a medical officer 'to provide food and medicines for diseased, destitute people at their own houses'.[14]

Figure 19: Lurgan Workhouse attic (1997 photo)

Unfortunately no reply to this letter exists, but its details illustrate both the alarming extent to which fever and its associated ailments had become endemic in the Lurgan area and the level of helplessness felt by concerned gentlemen like Hancock. However, any belief that the disease was rampant and could not be blamed on the authorities was challenged by two devastating and condemnatory investigations – one from within the workhouse, the other from without – which cast huge doubts over the competence of both the medical and administrative staff in that institution.

The deaths in the workhouse eventually reached the ears of the press and under the headline 'Mortality in Lurgan Workhouse' the *Newry Telegraph* reported on the 'frightful mortality' and the fact that many of the office-holders, as well as the paupers, had been, or were presently, ill.[15] *The Belfast Vindicator,* meanwhile, informed its readers that 'nearly 400 paupers have died in the Lurgan Workhouse during the last eight weeks.'[16] The Commissioners had also been monitoring the situation and obviously dissatisfied with the previous report of Dr. Bell, they decided to send Dr. Smith from the Central Board of Health to investigate workhouse conditions. The fact that Smith only visited two other workhouses, Bantry and Cork, and then made a trip of 300 miles northwards illustrates both the urgency which the Commissioners attached to the situation and their determination to effect a remedy as soon as possible.

Dr. Smith's report, completed on 17 February, concentrated on the standard of medical care in the workhouse but as a consequence it also offered an insight into the competence of the general administration therein. The most striking feature of the institution that emerged was the level of overcrowding, and Smith reported that in the male and female infirmaries there was an average of two persons to each bed, although three and four per bed was not uncommon.

The wards themselves were found to be in a terrible condition:

> There are four wards in the Idiot Department that are without any flooring but the earth, and in two of them there are no bedsteads, so that the beds lie upon the wet ground. One of them – in which at the time of my visit two wretched creatures were dying – was in an exceedingly foul condition; in one corner a pile of old filthy clothes, shoes, etc.; in another a large heap of straw; in another place a quantity of coals scattered about; the ventilation was very imperfect.[17]

Further investigation found the floors and walls of the infirmary to be in a 'very discreditable condition' with the windows almost

> universally closed, the atmosphere close and foul; the smell upon entering the rooms most offensive.[18]

Walls had not been white-washed, buckets, used as lavatories, were allowed to sit for hours without being emptied and medicines and drinks were served out on the floor where 'the boards were in a filthy state'. A similar scenario was presented to the doctor in the fever sheds. However, the fever hospital, controlled by a full-time nurse, was found to contain comfortable beds, clean walls and floors, well-ventilated wards and well-attended patients.

Due to general overcrowding it emerged that, as a result of an inadequate supply of garments, the clothes of those paupers who had died of fever or dysentery were used by other paupers without prior cleaning and drying.

Another area of concern was that of pauper burials. Evidently many paupers had been buried less than four yards from the Fever Hospital and in the centre of the burial ground was the well which supplied water to the workhouse. In fact, the graves had been dug so close to it that the water had become muddy and unfit for use. Not surprisingly, in the light of what he had witnessed, Smith described the Lurgan workhouse as 'a picure of neglect and discomfort such as I have never seen in any other charitable institution'. He thus recommended that the following measures be implemented as soon as possible:

1) All admissions to the workhouse to cease until fever and dysentery cases abate.

2) All rooms used by the sick to be properly fumigated and white-washed.

3) Movement of some patients from the infirmary to the workhouse where space was available.

4) Thorough whitewashing of the infirmary; cleansing of its floors and improvement of its ventilation.

5) Daily inspecton of the above recommendations to be carried out by the medical officer.

Alongside such improvements, Smith felt it necessary to apportion blame for the terrible conditions which he had enountered, and remarked:

> It is not difficult to deduce the causes of the mortality which has lately devastated the Lurgan workhouse and which still continues.[19]

He believed that the problems stemmed from the death of the master, John Meason, in early November and the fact that three weeks passed before a successor was appointed. During this period overcrowding had developed and continued until the end of January. This, coupled with the fact that many subordinate officers had been ill at one time or another, meant that

> ventilation, whitewashing and cleanliness appear to have been neglected at the very time when the strictest attention to these important means of arresting the spreading of disease were most imperatively called for.[20]

He contended that, despite a heavy workload, 'a little more activity' on the part of Dr. Bell, together with a stricter surveillance by the Guardians, would have prevented much of the mortality, stating:

> It appeared to me that the Guardians had no knowledge of the state of the infirmary as regards cleanliness, ventilation, etc. either from personal observation or otherwise. The reports of the physicians informed them of its overcrowded state and this was the only particular about it with which they seem to be acquainted.[21]

He concluded his report with the following indictment of the workhouse administration:

> I am of the opinion that the chief causes of the evil in question are internal, and the result of defective management of the institution.[22]

Such a wide-ranging report served to undermine the competence of those charged with caring for the paupers in the workhouse; but almost immediately afterwards a letter from one of the chaplains illustrated that there was a degree of negligence and indifference of an almost incredible nature amongst both staff members and the Board of Guardians.

In a lengthy letter to Lord Lurgan, the Rev. Oulton felt the need to draw his attention to the appalling standard of food being served in the workhouse:

> It is hardly to be wondered at that so much disease should be in the workhouse if the descripton of food has for any length of time been such as I saw there today.[23]

He said that the bread, used for supper, was dark-coloured, insufficiently baked, and sour, whilst the broth was so bad that many paupers could not use it. He described the meat as being

of the worst description that could be got in Lurgan Street –
more like the flesh of an animal that had died of disease than
being killed for food.[24]

Further, he doubted whether the cooking utensils and kitchen
were in an hygienic condition: 'It was once in a very bad state
and might be so again'. Oulton concluded his letter thus:

> I could not refrain from mentioning these matters to you which
> doubtless have had no inconsiderable share in producing the
> dreadful mortality which has sweeped our workhouse and I am
> sure you will take the earliest opportunity of investigating them
> to the utmost.[25]

Almost immediately an internal enquiry was convened by the
Board involving many of the principal workhouse officials. The
ward master, Thomas Lutton, said that the bread had been bad
for over a week and believed it to to be 'unfit for human food'.
He continued:

> Many of the sick paupers have complained to me that the bread
> was so bad they could not eat it and I consider their complaints
> are well founded.[26]

He said the the beef used for soup was of very poor quality and
reported this to Mr. Bullock:

> He said it had a very offensive smell but this soup was afterwards
> sent to the patients in the hospital.[27]

However, the stark contrast between the lives of the paupers and
those of the officers is illustrated by Lutton's following revelation:

> The bread furnished to the officers cannot be complained of
> and is much superior to what is provided for the paupers.[28]

This point was corroborated by another ward master, William
Fairly, who remarked:

> The baker, when he brings bread always has the officers' bread
> in a basket by itself.[29]

Fairly also believed the paupers' bread to be unfit for human
consumption – a view shared by Dr. Bell who believed the bread
to have been of poor quality for almost two months. Bell further
remarked that the meat had been 'defective' for a long time,
though never as bad as now, and concluded:

> I have no hesitation in stating that the disease in the house
> would not have been so bad if we had had a sufficient supply of
> wholesome bread and good beef such as was contracted for.[30]

Dr. McVeagh concurred with this opinion, believing that the
diarrhoea and dysentery now prevalent had been aided by the
use of sub-standard bread:

> From my experience as a medical man I don't know a worse
> description of food for persons affected with diarrhoea and
> dysentery than sour bread.[31]

The immediate consequence of the inquiry was the return of
200 lbs of bread to the contractor, Kennedy. However, John
Hancock, in a letter to the Commissioners, reported that only six
pounds of meat had been deemed to be unsound. He also offered
as a possible explanation for the obvious chaos in the workhouse
the fact that the master and matron both had fever and thus their
duties were being undertaken by the schoolmaster and mistress
who were 'doing their duty as well as can be expected under the
present trying circumstances'.

Regardless of any such excuses for the conditions in the
workhouse, the institution appears to have gained somewhat of a
notorious reputation in the Union which was reflected in the
following comment from Henry Wynne, Chairman of the Moira
Relief Committee:

> The mortality in the Poor House of Lurgan is such as would
> prevent our Guardians from sending any of our poor to the
> establishment at present.[32]

Unfortunately, on examining the sources, the revelations of
both enquiries do not come as a surprise. It is important to
remember that in February 1846, as noted in Chapter 3, a visiting
committee from the Poor Law Commissioners had described the
workhouse as being 'filthy and unclean'. Some months later Dr.
Stevens discovered conditions which, in his opinion, necessitated
an immediate removal of the medical officer. On the whole, the
Board of Guardians, together with some medical staff, appear to
have shown a complete disregard for the paupers under their
control. They made no attempt to ensure cleanliness and the

application of proper medical facilities. It seems incredible that the clothes of disease-ridden inmates, who had perished, were then passed, unwashed, to incoming paupers. Equally, no attempt was made to ensure a decent standard of food for the paupers. Indeed the use of unclean clothes together with supplies of bad bread and meat meant that, instead of ameliorating the spread of fever and other diseases, those in charge, through sheer incompetence, hastened the advance of mortality throughout the workhouse.

Dr. Smith pointed out that the significant lapse between the death of Mr. Meason and the appointment of a new master came at a time when the workhouse numbers were rapidly rising. In fact, between May 1845 and May 1847 there were no less than seven masters in the workhouse (see Table 5, Chapter 3). Such disruption would have done little to ensure the establishment of a smooth-running administration. However, this cannot excuse the inaction of other administrators. The fact remains that they had no idea as to what the conditions were in the workhouse and it took the reports of a visiting doctor together with the observations of a chaplain to bring the reality of the situation to their notice.

Consequently it is disconcerting to find that no one was prepared to shoulder the blame for the deficiencies and in fact only one member of staff resigned – Dr. Bell. In doing so, he reported that overworking had resulted in a deterioration of his health. However, regardless of such an explanation, it is unlikely that Bell would have been able to continue as medical officer after the scathing reports which had cast serious doubts on his professional competence. Consequently, the only course open to him was that of offering his resignation, which was accepted. Nevertheless, those charged with appointing both the medical and administrative staff and contracting for food did not feel the need to take similar action. There were no Board resignations or removals and in fact the only such change occurred in rather unfortunate circumstances.

Mortality and destitution did not prevail in the workhouse alone and a local newspaper gave the following account of conditions in the Lurgan area:

> Sickness is spreading rapidly outside the workhouse, and unless government immediately send down a medical gentleman from Dublin, to investigate the cause of the distemper, and take measures to check it, it will make an awful havoc here.[33]

This prediction proved to be correct as shortly afterwards the fever claimed its most high-profile casualty, the landlord Lord Lurgan, who died of typhus fever on 30 April. His sudden demise was lamented by the local press, with the *Newry Telegraph* declaring:

> He has ever been one of the most deservedly esteemed landlords in Ulster – paternal care and consideration for his tenantry he unceasingly manifested.[34]

For its part, the *Armagh Guardian* printed the following eulogy:

> The death of one whose charity and benevolence shed happiness and comfort on the neighbourhood in which he so constantly resided must not be passed over in silence. Constantly residing at his baronial mansion, he united daily with all classes of the people, patiently lending a ready ear to their distress, and ever mindful to their welfare.[35]

However the *Belfast Vindicator,* whilst regretting the late Lord's death, added a more sombre tone:

> When the concomitants of famine prey upon such victims, it is high time for the mighty and the wealthy to make common cause with the poor, and close the door against pestilence by shutting out hunger.[36]

Like all the mighty and wealthy members of society, Lord Lurgan was afforded a stately burial attended by local and national dignitaries as well as thousands of others. His body was interred in the Brownlow family vault in Shankill parish graveyard.

However, unlike the late Lord, those hundreds of paupers who perished in the workhouse and in the ditches, on the roads or in their pathetic mud-walled huts received no extravagant eulogies or burials. Indeed, Lord Lurgan's death received more attention in the press than any of the terrible occurrences in the workhouse. The paupers in that institution died in such quantities that the only testament to their existence was their number in the Book of Deaths which was painted on a label and placed at the head of each grave.[37] However, as the following report illustrates, they did not even receive the dignity of an individual burial:

> In the graveyard attached to the house, a large grave is made which fills nearly full of water a short time after it is opened. To its verge are brought the coffins containing the dead bodies – these coffins frequently contain two and three each – they are then put into the grave, in which they usually float. One or two persons then stand on the coffins in the water until the mould is heaped upon them. There are frequently twenty bodies in the one grave.[38]

Such indignity was not confined to workhouse burials and a member of the Society of Friends, commenting on conditions in Tartaraghan observed that,

> Last year, to have been buried without a hearse would have been a lasting stigma to a family; now hearses are almost laid aside.[39]

In later years it was claimed that among the fishing community, near Lough Neagh, a tradition of basket-weaving allowed for the development of basket coffins during this time. Owing to the distance involved in travelling to a graveyard from places such as the Bannfoot, near Charlestown, some people were buried in fields near their homes with the grave marked only by the planting of a sapling. Where there were several deaths in one family, the bodies were rolled in sacking and buried without coffins of any kind.[40]

The fact that death and disease were endemic in the Lurgan Union appears to have made little impact on the local press. In fact these papers, doubtless appealing to the middle and upper classes, appeared more interested in events in America, Europe and Africa than in the terrible occurrences much closer to home. Indeed, without the reports of various religious societies and the occasional letter to the press, one could easily be misled into believing that there was little distress in this area and that famine conditions were limited to Munster and Connacht. Such correspondence offers an insight into conditions in the Lurgan/ Portadown area during that terrible time.

The following letter to the *Belfast News Letter* from John Dilworth of Killicomaine, Portadown is a good example.

Sir,

Employed in administering the benevolence of Christian Friends in England, I have met with some most deplorable cases which, I think, cannot be exceeded even in the south of Ireland.

About the beginning of this month – April – on the old road leading to Portadown, I called on a family named McClean and found the house like a pig-sty. Having fled from the Lurgan Poor House, where fever and dysentery prevailed, they returned home only to encounter greater horrors. Want sent the poor man to bed and I gave him assistance, but he died a few days after. The wife, almost immediately after, met the same melancholy fate; and a daughter soon followed her parents to the grave.

On the Thursday after, I repeated my visit, and just within the door of the wretched habitation, I saw a young man, about twenty years old, sitting before a live coal, about the size of an egg, entirely naked; and another lad, about thirteen leaning against a post. On turning to the right, I saw a quantity of straw, which had become litter; the rest of the family reclining on this wretched bed, also naked, with an old rug for covering. The boy who stood against the post directed my attention to an object at my feet, which I had not seen before, and over which I nearly stumbled, the place being so dark – and oh! what a spectacle – a young man about fourteen or fifteen, on the cold damp floor, off the rubbish, dead!; without a single vestige of clothing, the eyes sunk, the mouth wide open, the flesh shrivelled up, the bones all visible, so small around the waist that I could span him with my hand. The corpse had been left in that situation for five successive days.

The same writer visited the house the following week and was presented with further horrors:

I put my shoulder to the door, pushed it again, and saw the same heap of rubbish and rug, under which lay two boys and a girl together. The young man, whom I had seen sitting at the coal in my preceding visit, now was dead upon the floor – thrown off the bed, and with his head close to that of the living one, his knees up to the face, the eyes and mouth wide extended. I asked the survivors how long had he been dead? In a hollow, sepulchral tone, they replied 'three days'. They seemed to be in a state of insensibility with respect to surrounding objects; and in this stupor I left them. Out of eight members of a family, three only now survive, and I understand that the doctor who has visited them through the past week states that none of these will be any time alive. This famine is stalking through our land, and pestilence in her train is accomplishing the work of destruction.[41]

Such harrowing and heart-rending sights were by no means uncommon. In Tartaraghan the Society of Friends reported that people had died of starvation and one member commented on seeing a four year-old girl, 'a few weeks ago a strong healthy girl, who was so emaciated as to be unable either to stand or move a limb'. Indeed such were the sights witnessed by the writer that he concluded:

We are, in short, rapidly approaching, and if unassisted, must arrive at a state parallel to the worst pictures that have been presented to the public from the county of Cork.[42]

However, conditions did not degenerate to such a level due largely to the fact that the Board of Guardians, under scrutiny by the Commissioners, quite literally began to get their house in order. On appointing a new medical officer, Dr. McLaughlin from Downpatrick, they decided to revise and improve all aspects of workhouse administration. From now on, the medical officer had to attend each Board meeting and present weekly reports of sickness, mortality, medical requirements and dietaries. Further, the master was now required to have his books written up and given to the clerk each Tuesday morning for posting to the Commissioners that evening. He was also required to attend each Board Meeting 'with all the necessary books of the establishment under his control for the information of the Board'.

Obviously taking account of Dr. Smith's comments, sanitary improvements were implemented: the porter was ordered to burn the clothes of deceased paupers and to fumigate with brimstone and sulphur the clothes of those still alive; all ventilators were to be cleaned and improved and 'lids with hinges placed on all the night stools'.

On March 24, Dr. Phillips was informed that his services were no longer required and on Dr. McLaughlin's orders, the Board refused admission to any further cases of fever and dysentery until further notice.[43]

A significant event occurred towards the end of March when Assistant Poor Law Commissoner, Mr. Senior, witnessed men and women helping themselves to food in the kitchen, unsupervised. He accused the master of being negligent, adding that he did not believe he would prove to be an efficient officer. Not surprisingly perhaps, the master, Mr. Easton, resigned shortly afterwards. His replacement, Charles Hinde, was appointed and resigned within a week and was in turn replaced by David Gillespie, who had previously been assisting the medical officer. Gillespie was appointed on a temporary basis but was made permanent master a short time later.[44]

With the appointment of a new master and medical officer, together with administrative and sanitary improvements, the workhouse began to operate more efficiently and this was evidenced by a significant reduction in the numbers dying. However, in early April the medical officer reported typhus fever as being 'very much on the increase' and on 1 May, the weekly Board meeting was held at the local courthouse. Perhaps mindful of Lord Lurgan's fate, the Guardians preferred this building to that of the workhouse where there was a 'prevalence of fever'. On receipt of a letter from Dr. Hannay of the Lurgan Dispensary informing them of the situation in Lurgan and Brownlowsderry, the Central Board of Health dispatched tents, marquees and bedding to those areas from ordnance stores at Charlemont.[45]

On 22 May and 7 June permission was granted for the erection of temporary fever hospitals at Moira, Magheralin, Lurgan,

Kernan (in Bullock's field), and Portadown, which between them provided beds for 225 patients. Such accommodation proved insufficient, however, and by 17 June, the medical officer reported sickness 'prevailing to a great extent – the fever and dysenteric apartments quite full and incapable of receiving more patients'.[46] Thus, as a matter of urgency, extra sheds and tents were provided with the establishment of fever hospitals on the Portadown Road, Lurgan and in Portadown itself – both of which catered for 200 patients.[47]

June also witnessed the introduction of the Temporary Relief Destitute Persons Ireland Act, more commonly known as the 'Soup Kitchen Act'. This move was significant in that the provision of gratuitous outdoor relief had previously been opposed by the government. Indeed, it was forbidden under the Poor Law Act of 1838 and had not been included in any of the temporary measures introduced since 1845. However, given the conditions of the time, it was regarded as an exceptional measure which would be strictly temporary in nature. Unlike the 'workhouse test', applicants for the relief did not have to be destitute, with four different categories being designated as eligible:

1. destitute, helpless or impotent persons
2. destitute persons not holding land
3. able-bodied persons holding small portions of land
4. employed, able-bodied persons whose wages were insufficient to maintain their families were allowed to purchase rations.

The relief provided was soup which was meant to be 'miserable and scanty', consisting of liquid, thick or thin, composed of meat, fish, vegetables, grain or meal. In addition, those applying received either 1½ lb of bread, or 1lb of biscuit, flour grain or meal.

Local relief committees were required to compile lists of people who were eligible to receive rations. People named on the relief list had to attend the soup kitchen on a daily basis bringing with them a suitable container for receiving the rations. The only exception to this were the sick or impotent poor, who were allowed to receive up to two weeks' rations at a time.

Table 7 illustrates the degree of dependence on relief under this Act in the Lurgan Union. In total, the maximum number dependent on relief was 8.2 percent of the population – a figure which meant that Lurgan was among the ten unions with least dependence. This compares with the highest figure of 94.4 percent for Ballinrobe, Co. Galway.[48]

Only nine of the nineteen electoral divisions in the Union came under the Act. This does not imply, however, that the other ten were not providing relief. Soup kitchens which had been established throughout the Union since December 1846 continued to be run on a private basis, funded by local subscriptions.

Table 7: Population dependent on relief scheme

Area	Number	% of Population
Ballyleny	187	9.5
Carrowbrack	408	14.9
Donaghcloney	489	22.5
Kernan	601	11.7
Moira	258	6.2
Portadown	1,343	18.8
Tartaraghan	1,362	30.2
Tullylish	712	13.6
Waringstown	441	9.7

Source: Reprinted Parliamentary Papers, Famine Series Vol. vii

The new Act was to be financed from the poor rates, although in the first instance, the government was willing to make advances on the security of local rates. Many residents, opposed to further increases in rates, refused to come under the scheme. Indeed, it is interesting to note that no divisions in the Lurgan area joined the scheme, whereas over half that did join were in the Portadown area. This is probably a reflection of Woodhouse's complaint that there was little or no relief work to be had in that vicinity. Tartaraghan, a couple of miles outside Portadown, had a level of 30.2 percent, making it the area most dependent on relief. Given the reports of the Rev. Clements this is hardly surprising since absentee landlords and lack of worthwhile relief initiatives meant that the populace suffered particularly badly. Furthermore, the figures demonstrate the wide diversity of dependence on the soup kitchen scheme, emphasising the localised impact of the Famine, even within particular Poor Law Unions.

The issuing of gratuitous relief under this scheme ended on 15 August, the government believing that by this time a new harvest would eradicate the need for such relief. Also, the Poor Law Extension Act came into effect in June, permitting Poor Law Guardians to provide relief outside of the workhouse for the first time. The Lurgan Guardians, with mounting debts, determined however to oppose any new measures which would serve to exacerbate their already precarious financial position.

Footnotes

1. Board of Guardians' Minute Book, 1847, pp. 321-391.
2. *Ibid.* pp. 401, 411, 421.
3. Lurgan Union Workhouse, Chaplains' Notebook, January/February 1847, (P.R.O.N.I. BG. 22/FO).
4. Board of Guardians' Minute Book, 1846, pp. 426-61.
5. *Ibid.* p. 426.
6. *Ibid.* pp. 431, 441, 451, 461.
7. Correspondence relating to the state of Union Workhouses in Ireland, Third Series, H.C., 1847 (863), vol. lv., pp. 5-23.
8. *Newry Telegraph,* 30 January 1847.
9. Board of Guardians' Minute book, 1846, pp. 435-56.
10. *Ibid.* p. 450.
11. *Ibid.* pp. 449-59.
12. *Ibid.* pp. 450-60.
13. Hancock to Mr Hanley, 15 February 1847, Letter Book of John Hancock, p. 309, (P.R.O.N.I. D1817/2).
14. *Ibid.* p. 309.
15. *Newry Telegraph,* 9 February 1847.
16. *Belfast Vindicator,* 10 March 1847.
17. Dr Smith, Report to the Board of Health, Dublin, on the state of the Lurgan Union Workhouse, H.C., 1847, (247) LV.ii, pp. 13-14.
18. *Ibid.* p. 14.

19. *Ibid.* pp. 14-16.
20. *Ibid.* p. 15.
21. *Ibid.*
22. *Ibid.*
23. Board of Guardians' Minute Book, 1846, p. 469.
24. *Ibid.* p. 469.
25. *Ibid.*
26. *Ibid.* p. 470.
27. *Ibid.*
28. *Ibid.*
29. *Ibid.*
30. *Ibid.* pp. 470-76.
31. *Ibid.* p. 477.
32. Henry Wynne to R.J. Routh, 5 February 1847, Relief Commission Papers.
33. *Belfast Vindicator,* 10 February 1847.
34. *Newry Telegraph,* 1 May 1847.
35. *Armagh Guardian,* 11 May 1847.
36. *Belfast Vindicator,* 1 May 1847.
37. Board of Guardians' Minute Book, 1846, p. 419.
38. *Belfast Vindicator,* 28 April 1847.
39. Transactions of the Central Relief Committe of the Society of Friends during the famine in Ireland in 1846 and 1847; Appendix III; p. 192.
40. Evidence of James Donnelly to the Irish Folklore Commission, 1945. Ms. 1069.
41. *Belfast News Letter,* 2 April 1847.
42. Society of Friends, Appendix III, p. 192.
43. Board of Guardians' Minute Book, 1846, pp. 509-38.
44. Board of Guardians' Minute Book, 1847, pp. 9, 10, 267, 550.
45. T.N. Redington to Ordnance officers, 13 May, 1847; C.S.O.R.P. Earl of Clarendon Letters, pp. 347-354, National Archives, Dublin.
46. Board of Guardians' Minute Book, 1847, p. 65.
47. Appendix A, to Third Report from the Relief Commissioners, p. 13, H.C., 1847, (836), vol. xvii;
48. Appendix iii to Fourth Report from the Relief Commissioners, p. 26, H.C., 1847, (859), vol. xviii; Appendix iii to Fifth Report from the Relief Commissioners, p. 22, H.C., 1847-8, (876), vol xxix.

6.

A Bankrupt Union

In December 1846, John Hancock had alluded to the fact that payments of rent were coming in slowly and that financial difficulties could result. The following months, when the Union had to cope with large numbers in the workhouse and provide money for relief committees and soup kitchens, exacerbated the situation and by mid-March 1847, the Union treasurers, the Ulster Bank, complained of an 'unusually large balance to the debit of the Poor Law account'. The extent of the difficulties was attested to by letters from Hancock to the Provincial Bank, Belfast. Remarking on what he termed 'the lamentable failure of the potato crop', he informed the bank that arrears were much greater than usual and rents were coming in 'very slowly'. The following extract, in which he compares 1847 with the previous year, demonstrates the strain which the potato failure placed on the Union resources:

> This time twelve months there was £2,442 of arrears of rent and now there are £6,064. This time twelve months I had £1,400 of his Lordship's in my hand and he owed the bank nothing. This year I have nothing in my hands and he owes £800 to the bank.[1]

By 24 June, the Ulster Bank was once again complaining of the large balance against the Union, which had now increased as a consequence of the building of the fever sheds and tents in the

Union – necessitating a loan of £1,600 from the Exchequer Loan Commissioners.

Attention had obviously been drawn to the size of the debt as on 8 July the Board received a letter from the Commissioners urging the necessity of a 'vigorous collection of the poor rate'.[2]

Unlike their replies to the demands of the bank, which were rather abrupt and dismissive, the Board felt that a full explanation of their financial position was necessary for the Commissioners. Their communication offers a further insight into the widescale suffering of the general population:

> There are in this Union a great proportion of the ratepayers or rather of occupiers liable to rates, whose sole dependence for the support of their families at this moment is a loom and nearly the entire amount of their furniture a bed, often of a most wretched description, with only one or two cooking utensils. On these the collector may lay his hands in default of payment but what must follow? Struggling industry will be driven forth upon the world, the addition of an entire family made to the paupers' list and a few shillings collected at the eventual expense of as many pounds.[3]

Offering these views as being 'the deliberate conviction of men resident in the country whose dearest interests are bound up in its condition', the Board conceded that they did not know the day the Bank would refuse them any advances, concluding:

> We would emphatically state the fact that the money which seems likely to be required at our hands is not at present in the County.[4]

Not only was money in short supply, but workhouse expenses were also continuing on an upward spiral. From March until September 1846 the maintenance costs totalled £1,010-10-1d whilst funerals cost £20-19-5d. However the following six-month period witnessed huge increases: maintenance was now £1,903-13-7d and funerals £124-13-10d. This pattern continued until 1850 by which time, with the crisis over, figures resembled their 1846 level.[5]

As a consequence, the Board was reported to be in 'very great difficulties' with their creditors on 2 September, due to the fact that 'little or no money' had been received in the previous two months. The following week the Ulster Bank informed them that no more advances would be authorised. As a matter of urgency, the clerk was told to make representations to the Northern and Belfast bank branches to enquire into the possiblity of opening an account. Further to this, Edward Senior was called upon to write to the Lord Lieutenant to explain in detail the extent of the problems in the Union:

> There is a debt to the Union Treasurer of £1,250 and a further sum due to contractors for provisions payable on Thursday next of upwards of £1,000. In addition to these debts, the cost of the Fever Hospitals under the Fever Act is £120 weekly. At the same time the cost of the provisions for the workhouse is weekly upwards of £80.[6]

In asking for a loan of £2,000, he went on to explain the consequences if the request were not met:

> I fear that the Guardians must close the Fever Hospitals, now containing upwards of 500 patients, besides throwing the Union into a position of extreme difficulty.[7]

However, the Commissioners did not feel disposed to help, saying that they could not encourage a system of borrowing which was not sanctioned by Parliament. They concluded by stating that, in their opinion 'no difficulty should exist in collecting rates in the Lurgan Union at the present period'.[8]

Fortunately for the Guardians, and presumably after much persuasion, the Belfast Bank offered the Union a loan of £2,000, which was gratefully accepted by the Board. Problems were further eased when the Relief Commissioners, doubtless made aware of the Union's problems, decided to forgo payment for temporary fever accommodation and changed the loan for such purposes into a grant. The response of the Board was to offer 'their unanimous expression of thanks to the lords of the Treasury for their great kindness in granting such a boon to the ratepayers in this trying season'.[9]

Although loans and grants helped to alleviate short-term financial difficulties, the fact remained that the Union could not balance its books and was spending much more than it was receiving. Consequently a more vigorous rate collection policy was adopted, with each Guardian being requested to act as an example to his area and pay his rates in full – with the 'disagreeable necessity' of legal proceedings being threatened if he did not do so. In a rather desperate move, the Board also resolved not to pay any contractor his dues until his rates had been paid in full – hence the Ulster Railway Company was told to pay their rates 'forthwith'.

Perhaps not surprisingly, this tougher policy was not well received. Writing from Magheralin, Robert Molly believed that 'serious resistance' was intended against the collection of a rate.[10] Further to this a large meeting was held at Shane's Hill, Tullylish 'for the avowed purpose of giving opposition to the collection of the poor rates'.[11]

More ominous was the following notice which was circulated throughout the same area by a figure calling himself 'Tommy Downshire':

> BRETHREN – Oppression calls me once more among you. Having heard of the dreadful high poor-rates imposed upon you, I warn you not to pay any more than 10d. in the pound. Any man giving more I will order him to be burned to the ground. Let them go to the landlords for the rest. I will go through the townlands shortly. Be firm and true – I will mind what the landlords are doing when I come. Let no-one dare to tear this notice down.[12]

Indeed the *Banner of Ulster* suggested that Downshire's 'satellites' would not hesitate 'to use the torch or the bullet against those who might disobey his orders'.[13] Such strength of feeling emanated from the recent huge increases in the rate – a direct result of having to cope with the Famine. Table 8 gives an indication of the rate rises in each area between 1846 and 1848. Eight areas experienced a rate increase of between five and nine hundred percent.

Table 8: Changes in Rating in the Lurgan Union, 1846-48

Rate per Pound (Pence)	1846	1847	1848
Lurgan	10	15	30
Cornakinnegar	5	10	5
Brownlowsderry	5	15	25
Carrowbrack	5	10	25
Kernan	5	10	45
Montiaghs	5	10	15
Tartaraghan	5	10	40
Drumcree	5	5	20
Breagh	5	5	15
Portadown	15	10	45
Aghalee	5	15	5
Aghagallon	5	15	20
Ballinderry	5	10	5
Moira	5	10	10
Tullylish	10	20	60
Magheralin	5	15	20
Ballyleny	5	5	5
Waringstown	10	5	20
Donaghcloney	5	10	40

Source: Lurgan Union Board of Guardians' Minute Books.

Whether as a result of the anger at such increases, or just the sheer inability of people to pay, by late October 1847 only £1,979 had been collected out of a total poor rate of £10,000 struck in mid-September.[14]

These financial difficulties appear to have had a major impact on the judgment of the Board, with the result that it soon came into conflict with the Commissioners.

In August, two of the Guardians, Hancock and Cuppage, in an attempt to alleviate overcrowding in the workhouse, forwarded a motion for the authorisation of outdoor relief in the Union for a period of two months. However when the matter was put to a vote, everybody else opposed the idea. Shortly afterwards, Assistant Commissioner Senior recommended the use of outdoor relief, with the stipulation that it be confined to the old, infirm and disabled. Given Mr. Senior's position, the Board decided to treat this idea with more respect and asked each Guardian to examine the particular requirements of his area and to report as to whether or not such relief was required. Considering the overwhelming vote against the earlier motion of Hancock and Cuppage, there seems little doubt that the Guardians would have remained opposed to relief. This point appears to have been recognised by the Commissioners who, dissatisfied with the Board's mode of enquiry, ordered them to appoint officers to supervise relief 'without delay'. However the Board remained resolute and in a letter to the Commissioners, in which they claimed to be the 'best judges' of the situation, they argued that the expense of appointing relieving officers was precluded by the present state of their finances; they also pointed to the fact that additional accommodation meant that 1,200 paupers could now be retained in the workhouse. Not surprisingly therefore when the reports from the Guardians of each area emerged, it was argued that no outdoor relief was required. Given their implacable opposition and the state of their finances, then described as being 'as embarrassing as can be imagined', this outcome was predictable. It is difficult to ascertain the level of local destitution at this juncture; it was probably not as bad as it had been earlier in the year, but there was still widespread suffering. Regardless of this, the Guardians seemed determined to take such vital decisions, not on the basis of local need, but in the light of the financial implications in establishing a system of relief:

> We consider it absolutely necessary to pause before imposing any further burdens upon our... exhausted resources for the appointment of any paid officers whose services are not required.[15]

Aside from the financial implications of such relief, there also appeared to be a fear amongst landowners that the initiation of this policy would lead to increased dependence on the state by those in need.

In a petition to the Lord Lieutenant, the landlords and gentry of Moira stated their opinion thus:

> Such a mode of relieving the labouring classes would, to a great extent, destroy the spirit of independence which your petitioners humbly conceive to be a necessary ingredient in the character of a useful, willing and proper class of labourers. That it would

lead to idle and improvident habits, and ultimately to the ruin of every class of persons in Ireland.[16]

A similar statement had been made earlier in the year by Lord Lurgan to the Lurgan Union Farming Society, in which he reiterated that they 'should not abandon the high and independent character of farmers to become beggars upon Government for money'.[17] Hence, it is plausible to contend that the unrestrained opposition of the Guardians to outdoor relief was as much concerned with a political ethos as with financial considerations. Apparently the gentry feared that if the labourers were given free food, this would increase their dependency on the authorities, creating what may be termed a 'proto welfare state'. To those opposed to such a move, it had to be avoided at all costs.

Hence, when Hancock and Cuppage proposed the division of the Union into six relieving districts, each served by a relieving officer, they were defeated by 17 votes to 2. However, on 2 December, the Commissioners ordered the Board to create six such districts – Lurgan, Portadown, Waringstown, Moira, Montiaghs and Tartaraghan – together with a relieving officer for each. At a Board meeting, Hancock and Cuppage, in an attempt to compromise, argued that although the workhouse did offer the best method of relief and outdoor relief was expensive, it would be best to appoint relieving officers, though for as short a time as possible. The majority restated their conviction that the workhouse was adequate to meet all needs, and indeed that in the short term, demands for relief would actually abate:

> There is, we trust, a likelihood of the linen trade reviving which will take a number of families off our hands.[18]

Thus, the Board adopted the position that,

> the moment has not yet arrived for entailing upon the pauperised and almost ruined ratepayers of this Union the additional burden of six paid officers.[19]

Such a decision, in direct contravention of their orders, was the last straw for the Commissioners and in a letter to the Board, they threatened the Guardians with immediate legal action for 'neglecting to appoint relieving officers'.

Faced with the humiliation of court proceedings, the Board capitulated in its opposition to outdoor relief. At an extraordinary meeting on 20 December, they voted to proceed to the election of six relieving officers on 6 January 1848.[20]

Thus 1847 ended as it had begun and continued, with the Board of Guardians being scrutinised by, and in conflict with, the Poor Law Commissioners. The machinations of the Poor Law had little relevance to the daily lives of those who depended on it, however. For the poor of the Lurgan Union, obtaining a daily meal was their only concern and their plight was stressed by the report of death by starvation of a man named Jarden in Ballyblough, on the outskirts of the town on 26 December.[21] The year 1848 was thus looked to with a sense of foreboding.

Footnotes

1. Hancock to Provincial Bank, Belfast, 27 February 1847, Letter Book of John Hancock, p. 310.
2. Board of Guardians' Minute Book, 1847, p. 96.
3. *Ibid.* p. 98.
4. *Ibid.* p. 98.
5. Abstracts of the Accounts of the Lurgan Union, 1841-50, BG22/CJ/1, P.R.O.N.I.
6. Edward Senior to the Poor Law Commissioners, 30 September, 1847. C.S.O.R.P. No. 31,437 D/47, National Archives, Dublin.
7. *Ibid.*
8. T.N. Redington to Ordnance officers, 13 May, 1847; C.S.O.R.P. Earl of Clarendon Letters, pp. 347-354, National Archives, Dublin.
9. Board of Guardians' Minute Book, 1847, pp. 77, 237, 240, 250.
10. Molling to Dublin Castle, 26 October 1847, Outrage Papers.
11. *Ibid.* 8 November 1847.
12. *Banner of Ulster*, 15 October, 1847.
13. *Ibid.*
14. Board of Guardians' Minute Book, 1847, p. 26.
15. *Ibid.* pp. 266-267.

16. *Northern Whig,* 13 March 1847.
17. *Newry Telegraph,* 25 February 1847.
18. Board of Guardians' Minute Book, 1847, pp. 310-40.
19. *Ibid.* p. 330.
20. *Ibid.* p. 340.
21. *Ibid.* p. 376.

7.
Signs of Recovery

In some parts of the country, the Famine continued until 1852. However, the generally accepted opinion is that 1847 witnessed the worst of the suffering, hence the often-used phrase 'Black 47'. Although this may be correct in terms of fatalities, it would appear to be an oversimplification of the situation. Indeed, if anything, distress in the Lurgan Union actually increased in 1848, but the major difference was that the authorities were in a much better position to deal with it.

In November 1847, the Guardians came to an agreement with George Greer, one of their number, that part of his distillery (see Figure 20) in the Back Lane (now North Street) be rented for one year at a cost of £150.

This building, with accommodation for more than four hundred inmates, was fitted-out as an auxiliary workhouse containing dormitories, a dining hall and schoolrooms. Initially only the boys from the main workhouse were sent to the distillery, but by the end of December they had been joined by the girls. This had the effect of reducing the pressure of numbers in the main workhouse.

However, the distillery was only a temporary arrangement and the Guardians realised that permanent changes to the workhouse were required. In January 1848 John Hancock recommended the setting up of a building committee to consider various proposals. Following consultation with Messrs Senior and Wilkinson (the original architect) it was decided to construct convalescent wards catering for one hundred inmates, adjacent to the fever hospital. More new buildings for children were to be erected on each side of the entrance buildings, the contract for the work, amounting to over £3,000, being awarded to John Brown of Belfast. Having learnt harsh lessons during the previous year, the Guardians were not going to take any further risks, regardless of the costs. They had seen how the workhouse with a capacity of 800 had proved totally inadequate to cope with the needs of the Famine, being completely overwhelmed in the early months of 1847. However, with the addition of the distillery, together with temporary fever hospitals, total relief capacity was now over 1,500.[1]

The acquisition of more space was vital as in the early months of 1848 the numbers requiring relief remained above 1,200, reaching a peak of 1,365 in the week ending February 16.[2] For those who believe that 1847 saw the worst of the crisis, such figures require explanation.

One of the consequences of the 1846 blight was that only a tiny amount of seed potatoes remained to be planted for the following year. Hence, although ironically the 1847 crop was largely unscathed, it was only a fraction of what was required. Therefore, for many people the problem in 1848 was the same as in the previous year – an acute shortage of their staple diet.

However, of equal significance in this area was the fact that a slump in the linen industry continued, and indeed worsened, in the new year. In February, a resident of Portadown wrote:

> We have much cause of thankfulness for the business we have, considering the unprecedented want of employment and means of earning money. The linen trade has been very dull with almost no weaving and hundreds of looms lying idle. Only that provisions are cheap we would be worse than last year.[3]

Indeed the prices of crops such as grain, meal, and oats had dropped dramatically in a year, being approximately one-third of the rate they had attained in the early months of 1847. Consequently, one retailer in Portadown remarked that the shop business was 'deplorably bad',[4] while John Hancock observed:

> The middle classes are in greater distress this year than last.
> Trade is flat and credit has nearly left the country.[5]

Hence, although the fall in prices may have enabled some to
obtain food, and thus proved a mitigating factor in terms of
fatalities, distress was more widespread in 1848. The agricultural
slump eventually hit those who had successfully navigated the
previous year: farmers who owned around twenty acres and
depended on a good market for their livelihood.

John Montgomery of Portadown remarked as follows:

> Small farmers in this country are nearly bankrupt – produce so
> low and taxes so high – they cannot live, and all over the land
> there have been thousands of ejectments taken out by landlords
> and hundreds of farms for sale.[6]

In his comments he referred to another problem for farmers.
With the poor rate being a local tax, it meant that areas requiring
most relief were taxed hardest. In this way a vicious circle was
created by which those liable for rates were themselves slipping
into debt, as Montgomery noted:

> Farmers, especially small ones have felt the pressure of the
> times and the poor rates are so high, and produce so low that
> many of them cannot go on unless a change comes somewhere
> – either rent and rates lower or prices higher.[7]

Indeed, it was claimed that in Portadown large quantities of
bed and bedding had been seized for payment of poor rates and
publicly auctioned.[8]

Recognising these difficulties, the 'landed proprietors' of
Tartaraghan, one of the worst affected areas, requested that the
Guardians defer payment of rates until the harvest 'in consequence
of the scarcity of money at present among the farming class there'.

However, given the financial difficulties faced in the previous
twelve months, the Guardians were adamant that no exemptions
be made and 'in justice to the rest of the Union and in safety to
ourselves' they refused to grant any such deferment.[9]

Nevertheless, some factors offered cause for optimism. Between
January and March there were 229 deaths in the workhouse.
Although still a large number it was less than half for the same

Figure 20: Distillery in North St, used as auxiliary workhouse (1978 photo)

period in 1847, while numbers in the workhouses were almost twice those of the previous year. Indeed, from April onwards the number of fatalities fell markedly and from then until the end of the year 156 deaths occurred. This period also saw the first week – ending June 24 – in which no deaths resulted, the first such since September 5, 1846.

Such had been the level of fatalities in 1847 that the workhouse graveyard had been filled to capacity. By August all those who died in the workhouse were buried in the Church of Ireland burial ground at Shankill graveyard. This trend continued until March 1848 when, after lengthy negotiations, the Guardians secured a new plot of ground near to the workhouse. Thus the acquisition of a new workhouse graveyard ensured that adequate space was now available for future burials.[10]

By April, the medical officer was able to report the workhouse to be 'in as healthy a state as it has been for a long time'. Similarly the house committee stated that the building was 'extremely clean and well kept and the paupers employed'. Throughout the Union it was reported that a large area had been planted with potatoes which were said to be doing 'very well'.[11] However an observer added a note of grim consequences if the crop were to fail:

> If it should please the Father of all flesh to again punish us for our sins by the loss of the potatoes, we must again pass through scenes similar to those of last year.[12]

The cautionary note proved apt as once again the crop was attacked by blight with the result that 'half the potatoes are unfit for man or beast'.[13]

However, the failure of the crop was offset by a welcome improvement in the linen trade, as noted by John Montgomery:

> The linen trade I believe is better, although many in it have gone down – the 'Smiths' of Banbridge, the 'Achesons' of Tandragee and others.[14]

The demise of some firms demonstrated the extent of the slump and another manufacturer, John Capper of Lurgan, whilst admitting losses approaching £150 in 1847, wrote as follows:

The linen trade made a little better for some months back... it is better than it has been for some time and there is some stir in the trade in Belfast.[15]

By the end of 1848 then, the linen trade was starting to revitalise itself and with weekly death-rates in the workhouse down to single figures, the signs were that the Union was on the road to recovery.

However, the new year was to herald another trauma for the poor of the area whilst the rate payers faced new increased burdens on their means.

Footnotes

1. Board of Guardians' Minute Book, 1847, pp. 310, 350, 459, 488-9.
2. *Ibid.* p. 1.
3. John Montgomery to Joseph Seawright, Portadown, 24th February 1848. Montgomery Papers D27941, 12/16 (P.R.O.N.I.).
4. *Ibid.* Robert Moore to Joseph Seawright, Portadown, 20th April 1848. D27941, 112/20.
5. John Hancock to the Lord Lieutenant, 21st April 1848. Outrage Papers (National Archives).
6. John Montgomery to Joseph Seawright, Portadown, 25th January 1849. D27941, 112/32.
7. *Ibid.* Portadown, 8th March 1849. D27941, 112/55.
8. *Newry Telegraph*, 6th March 1849.
9. Board of Guardians' Minute Book, 1848, pp. 89, 129.
10. *Ibid.* p. 129.
11. John Montgomery to Joseph Seawright, Portadown, 8th June 1848; D27941, 112/24.
12. *Ibid.*
13. John Montgomery to Joseph Seawright, Portadown, 19th October 1848. D27941, 112/27.
14. John Montgomery to Joseph Seawright, Portadown, 25th January 1849, D27941, 112/32.
15. John Capper to Joseph Seawright, Lurgan 26th October 1848, D27941, 112/28.

8.

Opposition to Rate-in-Aid

In the first week of January 1849 the workhouse medical officer issued the following report to the Guardians:

> I have to call the attention of the Board to the obnoxious atmosphere which surrounds the grounds of the workhouse. I would not have brought this circumstance before your notice had not a very suspicious case presenting all the symptoms of cholera occurred on Sunday night last, and which if it had not been seen as early as it was would no doubt have proved fatal. Of the certain approach of cholera I think very little doubt can exist.[1]

The doctor's sense of foreboding was doubtless grounded in the knowledge that reports of cholera in Belfast had been circulating in late December 1848. By February the *Belfast News Letter* reported the disease to be 'decidedly on the increase in this town – Belfast – and the immediate vicinity'.[2] The spread of the disease was also noted in Newry and Derry and the Guardians in Lurgan wasted little time in preparing for its arrival here. Local cholera committees were established in Seagoe, Lurgan and Drumcree, each supplied with a medical officer. Dr. Hannay also opened a dispensary for patients at his own residence in Lurgan. On March 29, he reported the first case of Asiatic Cholera in the town, which proved to be fatal.[3]

By early April a new ward, isolated from the rest of the workhouse, had been set aside for the reception of cholera patients.

It was soon filled. The major symptoms of the disease – diarrhoea and dysentery – were said to be 'very much on the increase', both inside and outside the workhouse. Many of those admitted from rural areas entered in a state of 'extreme collapse' and died within hours. Indeed, in one typical example, one of the nurses in the cholera ward took ill in the morning and died before midday.[4] Given that cholera thrived among open cesspools and sewers together with 'damp, filthy, uninventilated habitations' and 'improper food', it is no surprise that it found sustenance in this area.[5] As we have seen in Chapter 2, Doctors Shaw and Gilbert found many dwellings in Lurgan to be in an absolutely filthy condition.

By early September the epidemic was reported over with 369 cases and 116 deaths in Lurgan; for Portadown, the figures were 42 and 20 respectively.[6] Compared to the level of deaths in 1847 such figures are comparatively small and they proved the value of prompt action by the Guardians and medical staff. By ensuring proper treatment facilities, and confining the disease to one part of the workhouse, they succeeded in avoiding the huge mortality of two years previously.

For the most part, however, the Guardians were engaged in other matters which, in the long-term, they would probably have regarded as more important. In February 1849, the Whig Prime Minister, Lord John Russell, proposed to introduce a national rate of 6d in the pound to be imposed on every Poor Law Union in the country, with the exception of twenty-three bankrupt Unions, all of which, except Glenties, were in Connacht and Munster. Those who opposed this 'rate-in-aid' believed that the 'prosperous' areas of the North and East were to pay for the 'laziness' of the South and West. Indeed, as Jim Grant states:

> Ulster members of Parliament had no doubts about the superiority of their local Guardians... and they spread an Ulster propaganda within Parliament, whereby they conveyed the misleading impression that the rate would bear more heavily on Ulster than on any other province.[7]

Thus, the campaign against the rate was vigorously stated and nowhere more so than in the Lurgan Union.

On February 12, the first steps against the proposal were taken. A committee comprising William Blacker and four other Guardians prepared a petition to Parliament in which they greeted the proposal with 'intense alarm and dismay'. They believed that such a rate would be a tax upon 'the industrious of Ulster and Leinster for the support of idleness and improvidence in Munster and Connacht.' Believing the measure to be 'fraught with injustice and ruin', they determined to use 'every means in their power to avert it'.[8] It was agreed that a meeting of ratepayers and property owners be held in Lurgan on Friday 2 March at midday, for the purpose of preparing petitions to both Houses of Parliament. Their determination was attested to by the printing and posting of one thousand copies of their resolution throughout the Union.[9] Similar measures were taken in other Unions throughout the North and newspapers abounded with reports of 'anti rate-in-aid meetings', together with editorials and letters lambasting the proposal.

Inevitably the Lurgan meeting, which proved to be one of the largest, attracted widespread press coverage, with local papers carrying verbatim accounts of the speeches, some of which were extremely lengthy. The attendance was approximated at between three and four thousand and they heard each speaker emphasise two main points: firstly, the tax was unjust and should be imposed throughout the United Kingdom of Britain and Ireland; secondly, the 'industrious' people of Ulster should not be forced to pay for 'laziness' in Munster and Connacht.

William Blacker stated that he resented having to pay for what he termed the 'mismanagement of our neighbours', believing the measure to be only 'the point of the wedge' and that the tax would become permanent. He continued:

> I would observe that once upon a time, the sending of a man 'to Hell or Connacht' was considered a terrible denunciation. Things are now strangely altered. Verily, it would seem the best thing that can happen to a poor man is to betake himself to Connacht, hang up his hat and do nothing but hold his mouth open to be filled at the expense of Ulster.[10]

Charles Douglass similarly stated his opposition to aiding the 'mismanagement and idleness' of others:

> I think it unfair that England and Scotland should not bear their portion of the national calamity. Why not impose an Imperial rate? If they did, the people of Ulster would be ready to pay their share of it. I do not wish to see the industry of the North taxed for the idleness of the South and West, where, instead of attending to such matters as would serve them and their families, you would be told that Paddy was at a wedding and Biddy was at a wake.[11]

As far as Robert Dolling was concerned, the suffering in the West and South was self-inflicted and deserved no sympathy:

> It is very true that the potato has failed in Munster and Connacht, but it is also true that it has failed in Ulster, and why does that failure not affect the people of the North as it has done those of the South? Because the Northerners are a hardworking industrious people, and the blessing of God is upon their labours. If the people in the South had been as industrious as those in the North, they would not be in the condition they are in.[12]

For his part, John Woodhouse stated that he had first hand experience of the people of the West, finding them sitting by their firesides for six months in the year:

> They have so many days on which they cannot work; if there is a corpse to be buried in the townland, they cannot work. They also have so may saints' days to observe in the year. However, it all comes to this: everything is to be celebrated by a day's idleness. Go amongst them in the summer and you will find them lying stretched in the sun at the backs of the ditches, utterly refusing to work.[13]

The meeting concluded with the presentation of a petition signed by 4,800 ratepayers of the Union to be presented in both Houses of Parliament by Sir William Verner, MP for County Armagh.[14]

If we are to understand the views expressed in the speeches it is important to place them in the context of the events of the time. The introduction of a new tax, apparently only to last two years, was both feared and resented. Ten years previously the Poor Law had been introduced, ensuring that all ratepayers were now liable to pay for the relief of the poor of their area. However, as noted earlier, some areas suffered worse than others, resulting in severe rate increases and pressure on ratepayers. It was believed that this new tax would begin at 6d in the pound but then spiral upwards.

For many, the notion of a United Kingdom had no credence if an imperial rate was not imposed. It was felt that Devon and

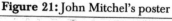

Figure 21: John Mitchel's poster

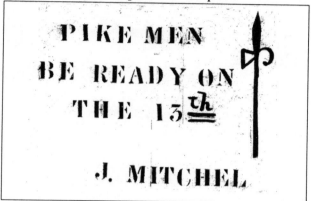

Cornwall had as much responsibility for areas in Clare and Galway, as the North did. The point was repeatedly made that, of the four provinces in Ireland, Ulster was by far the most loyal to the Queen and government; was this, therefore, how their loyalty was to be rewarded? Indeed that loyalty, they argued, had been further emphasised after the Young Ireland rebellion of 1848, which, although sporadic in nature, did have some reverberations locally. In April, supporters of John Mitchel, one of the leaders of the uprising, posted placards around Lurgan urging 'pikemen' to insurrection (see Figure 21). In August, after the failure of the rebellion and subsequent imprisonment of its instigators, a petition signed by more than fifty residents of Lurgan was sent to the Lord Lieutenant urging the release of William Smith O'Brien (see Figure 23), a member of the landed gentry and leader of the Young Ireland Movement. The rebellion also excited reaction amongst those loyal to the crown and on May 3 of that year, Charles Douglass had presented an address from the 'loyal inhabitants of Magheralin' to the Lord Lieutenant in which they expressed their 'detestation of the seditious proceedings of certain evil- minded individuals' and pledged 'allegiance to our beloved Queen... and determination to assist in maintaining order, suppressing outrage, and checking the progress of sedition'. A rate-in-aid was not what they had anticipated in return for such loyalty.[15]

While the rights and wrongs of the matter can be debated, there can be no doubt that a propaganda campaign was being waged. The impression was given that Ulster alone would have to shoulder any burden, but this was simply not true. Leinster had a higher poor law valuation: £4.75m as against £3.25m in Ulster. Thus the eastern province was to bear the heaviest burden of support. In relation to the constant references to the 'industrious men of the North' and 'mismanagement of the West', there is no doubt that many Unions in Ulster had coped well in times of distress. Indeed Edward Gulson, assistant Poor Law Commissioner, cited several Unions in the province as containing the best examples of workhouse administrations. In particular he noted Newtownards, Armagh, and Banbridge.[16] Significantly, though, Lurgan did not feature in his list. This is hardly surprising when one considers the problems it had in 1847. Dr. Smith, in his report, believed the huge mortality had been the result of 'defective management'. Furthermore, in his opinion, the Guardians had no knowledge of the state of the infirmary. Later in that same year the Guardians reported the Union to be 'in very great difficulties with their creditors', necessitating a loan of £1,600 being changed into a grant, as the Board could not repay it. Edward Senior, in reporting on the thirty-one Unions in his district on 24 March 1847, wrote of Lurgan as follows:

> This Union must become insolvent; not one-half the rate will be collected.[17]

Given, therefore, what had gone before, one could have expected that if any Board of Guardians was able to empathise with management and financial difficulties, it would have been the members of the Lurgan Board. Instead, we find in the speeches hypocrisy of the highest order. Douglass, Blacker, etc. appeared to either have short memories, or else preferred to forget the events of 1847. Greer and Dolling even had the audacity to claim that each Union should support its own poor, without receiving external aid – how, then, would the Lurgan Union have survived in 1847? If nothing else, they should have been able to understand how situations of bankruptcy could arise, and the difficulties in collecting rates from an impoverished tenancy. However, they chose to ignore such matters, and instead, seemed intent on belittling the starving people of the West and South with their vitriolic speeches. Not content with castigating those people for their perceived 'laziness' and 'indolence', they also, in Grant's words, 'touched the sectarian nerve'[18] a reference to Douglass' comment about the inactivity of 'Paddy and Biddy' and Woodhouses' about 'saints' days'. The *Belfast News Letter* in an editorial also alluded to this aspect of the debate with the following contribution:

Figure 22: Colonel William Blacker

> The sturdy men of the North will not now be compelled to feed
> the starving masses whom bad landlordism, disloyal teaching,
> a false religion and an inherent laziness have combined at once
> the share and canker of their country.[19]

Thus, the starving of the West and South were to be vilified not
least because they were Catholics.

Such comments did little for the cause against the rate but
showed that, as in many other aspects of everyday life,
sectarianism was not far from the surface. The Board of Guardians
had not encountered any such problems, probably because each
of its members was a Protestant. It is, however, interesting to note
that William Blacker invariably voted against any proposal
proffered by John Hancock, giving rise to the suspicion this may
have had something to do with the fact that Blacker was a leading
Orangeman whilst Hancock was a vehement opponent of the
movement. Indeed in the mid-1830s, when Orange marches were
barred by the Party Processions Act, Hancock prosecuted
Orangemen who had held an illegal demonstration in the grounds
of Blacker's demesne. His effigy was subsequently burned at
Orange marches.[20] It is also interesting to note that Hancock, one
of the most active public representatives of the time, was absent
from rallies against the rate – perhaps he was only too aware of
the rabble-rousing nature of these occasions. Nevertheless the
determined nature of the campaign was such that John
Montgomery wrote from Portadown:

> There have been meetings and petitions without end. How it
> will go I know not; most likely Lord John Russell will yield to
> the pressure from without, or very much alter it.[21]

Russell did not yield and all the meetings and petitions came to
nought. The government's proposal was passed in the House of
Commons by a vote of 206 to 34. On June 14 the Guardians
received a sealed order from the Commissioners for levying a
'general rate-in-aid of certain distressed Unions and electoral
divisions in Ireland'. The Lurgan Union's contribution was to be
£2,329 or a rate of 6d per pound on the Poor Law valuation of
£93,193.[22]

The intense debate over the rate-in-aid overshadowed a gradual and marked improvement in the fortunes of the Union during 1849. The linen industry had emerged from its slump and looms were introduced into the workhouse. Significantly the following entry appeared in the workhouse minute book on September 6:

> It appearing that abundance of potatoes of excellent quality are now to be had on moderate terms. Ordered that the clerk be directed to receive proposals for a supply to be provided daily as the return to this diet will be both economical and highly gratifying to the pauper inmates.[23]

Thus for the first time since September 1845, potatoes made a return to the diet of the workhouse, with adults receiving $3^1/_2$ lbs three days per week. With workhouse numbers at their lowest level in four years – averaging 430 per week – some semblance of pre-Famine 'normality' returned to the Lurgan Union.

Footnotes

1. Board of Guardians' Minute Book, 1848, pp. 405-6.
2. *Belfast News Letter*, 13th February 1849.
3. Board of Guardians' Minute Book, 1848, pp. 536-7.
4. *Ibid.* 1849, p. 125.
5. *Ibid.* p. 135.
6. Board of Guardians' Minute Book, 1849, p. 205.
7. James Grant 'The Great Famine and the Poor Law in Ulster: The rate-in-aid issue of 1849' in *Irish Historical Studies*, vol. XXVll. No 105 (May 1990), p. 30.
8. Board of Guardians' Minute Book, 1848, pp. 479-80.
9. *Ibid.* 1848, p. 480.
10. *Belfast News Letter*, 6th March, 1849.
11. *Ibid.* 6th March 1849.
12. *Armagh Guardian*, 12th March, 1849.
13. *Ibid.* 12th March 1849.
14. *Newry Telegraph*, 4th April 1848.
15. *Banner of Ulster*, 15th May, 1848.
16. James Grant, 'The Great Famine and the Poor Law in Ulster', pp. 33, 38.
17. Correspondence relating to the state of Union Workhouses in Ireland, Third Series. H.C., 1847 (863) Vol. lv. Appendix I, p. 2.
18. James Grant, 'The Great Famine and the Poor Law in Ulster', p. 33.
19. *Belfast News Letter*, 23rd February, 1849.

20. James Kane, *For God and the King*, Lurgan, Ulster Society, 1995, p. 88.

21. John Montgomery to Joseph Seawright, Portadown, 8th March 1849, D2794/1 12/35. Montgomery Papers (P.R.O.N.l.).

22. Board of Guardians' Minute Book, 1849, p. 116.

23. *Ibid.* 1849, p. 229.

Figure 23: Petition in support of William Smith O'Brien and other State Prisoners

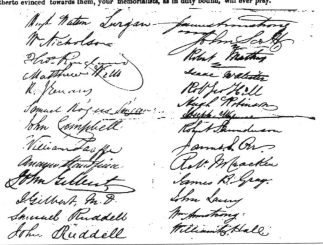

9.

'Happy Ulster'?

The previous chapters have outlined the extent of the Famine in the Lurgan Union in 1846-9. The degree of suffering endured by the population may surprise those who had previously believed that this area escaped relatively unscathed from the ravages of that time. Such a conception, still widespread, stems from the assumption that this area, as the centre of a thriving linen industry, could not possibly have suffered to the same extent as areas where industrialisation was limited. Thus, the argument goes, even if the potato failed, the population could rely on linen to support themselves in times of hardship. This hypothesis has some merit. Unfortunately, however, it places too much emphasis on the stability of the linen industry. What, for example, happened when linen went into a slump?

In 1846 Colonel Blacker stated that 'fifty or more labourers may be obtained for any job that may give a tolerable continuance of employment'. Crucially, however, he continued: 'If a depression in the weaving business occurs, double as many would be glad to be engaged'.[1]

Thus when a slump developed, weavers had to resort to whatever work was available in order to survive. If such a depression were to have emerged at the same time as the potato crop failed, would weavers have been any better-off in relation to the general, unskilled labourers living entirely on the potato?

Prior to the 1830s many of the stages of linen manufacture were domestic-based. Flax was grown on a plot of land attached to the house. The women then spun this into yarn which was woven into unbleached linen cloth by the males in the household. This brown cloth, as it was known, was then taken to market and sold to bleachers. However, in 1825 James Kay of Preston patented the wet-spinning process by which fine yarns could be spun much more economically than before. This innovation undermined the previous system of domestic spinning and ensured the gradual disintegration of home-made linen. A witness to the Commission inquiring into the condition of handloom weavers in 1840 commented as follows:

> Great loss has been sustained by the weavers' families being thrown idle owing to the substitution of the mill yarn. Formerly a hand spinner would get four to four and a halfpence a hank ... and now they get one to one and a halfpence, even if they could get the yarn to spin, which they frequently cannot. The machinery has thrown our families idle.[2]

The natural corollary of this development was that yarn was now in the hands of large-scale manufacturers. Thus weavers, instead of using their own yarn, now had to negotiate with businessmen before beginning to weave. They also had to agree a set price for any piece of finished cloth and were subject to fines for either not completing work on time or for faults in their cloth. Apprenticeships thus represented a risk that few were willing to take. In this way the new 'putting-out' system undermined the traditional independence of handloom weavers. One weaver from County Armagh, in a submission to the 1840 Commission, lamented the decline of his craft:

> The weavers generally are so poor that they cannot weave for the market as they formerly did but are compelled to take work from the manufacturers at whatever they can get. This increase of manufacturers has very much lessened the earnings of the poor; it has also produced a competition among them which has reduced prices and with it wages. The average earnings of all our weavers would not exceed three shillings and sixpence a week and that is with an attendant as winder.[3]

Thus, for areas such as Drumcree, Shankill and Seagoe, where 'nearly the entire population was composed of weavers,'[4] the years immediately prior to the Famine were characterised by technological innovation which undermined their economic well-being.

A further determinant of the weavers' livelihood was the general market conditions of the time. If the economy was healthy and demand for goods high, then the weavers survived; if not, they struggled.

In the vital year of 1847, commentators have referred to what they term a 'commercial crisis'.[5] This period was one of much railway construction and peaks in this industry were counterbalanced by a slackening in export industries, particularly textiles.[6] One such peak occurred in 1847 with the result that linen and cotton went into slump. As a consequence, construction of new mills in Belfast was halted. Those partially built were left unfinished, whilst some which had been built were not filled with machinery.[7] So serious was the situation that in May, in an editorial entitled 'The Money Crisis', the *Northern Whig* proclaimed that

> productive industry is paralysed and the working population are thrown out of employment and left dependent on charity.[8]

The plight of the previously relatively prosperous weavers is illustrated by the comments of Edward Sands at a meeting at Shane's Hill, Tullylish in May 1848.

> I've wove the ould diaper many a day and got 4d a yard for it; but now I can only get a penny a yard and can't get enough of it at that. I can't stand it any longer. I would like to make an honest living, as I have always done and always will do, with the help of God; but when it comes home to a man's self and he can't even get one meal of Indian stirabout in the day – some days a sheal, and some days none – how can he live?[9]

A fact often overlooked by Famine historians is that the potato was not the only crop to suffer in 1846-7. In early January 1847, the *Northern Whig* reported that the oat crop was 'much more deficient than was at first calculated upon'. In fact it proved to be less than half that expected, and the subsequent shortfall resulted in significant price increases. In August 1846 crop prices (per

cwt.) were as follows: Oats, 9/-; Oatmeal, 14/-; Barley, 8/-. By
February 1847, prices had risen to: Oats, 15/6d.; Oatmeal, 25/;
Barley, 16/-.

Allied to this was a sub-standard flax crop. In July of the
previous year, 1846, the same paper observed that the new crop
had been attacked with 'some vegetable distemper'. In March
1847, a correspondent reported:

> Flax is so dear and scarce that it cannot be had, even if the
> spinners could afford to pay the very highest prices.[10]

The Belfast markets were testament to such problems and flax
was said to exist in very small quantities with 'scarcely any good
lots of either hand or milled'.[11] Hence, the unlikely combination
of a slump in demand, together with poor flax and oat harvests,
served only to accentuate the problems already being experienced
by weaving communities.

It must be remembered that in such communities linen did
offer an alternative to agriculture. As such it removed many
barriers to early marriage, thus creating the potential for large
families. This point can stimulate much debate. However, the
fact remains that areas of linen manufacture were among the
most densely populated in Ireland. The most populous of these
was the North Armagh area – bounded by Lurgan Poor Law
Union. Lord Lurgan owned 24,600 acres in Armagh and this was
inhabited by 23,800 people. Much of this land was bog, and yet,
on average, 511 people occupied each square mile. The majority
of these depended on linen for their livelihood; however, in 1846-
7, it did not provide them with security against a complete failure
of the potato crop. The following report from Tartaraghan
illustrates the gravity of the situation.

> The weaver at present can only earn two shillings and sixpence
> to four shillings and sixpence by weaving a web of sixty yards,
> which employs him nearly a whole week in preparation: while
> at present prices such wages will not support the mere weaver
> without a family. Even with such wages I can state it as a fact ...
> that weavers are sitting up three nights per week, in order by
> any means to procure food for their families. In several cases,
> I have relieved individuals at their own houses who from

exhaustion had been compelled to lie down and could no longer continue at work on the loom.[12]

The severity of the weavers' predicament was encapsulated in the author's conclusion: 'Even this mode of scanty and insufficient employment is rapidly ceasing'.[13]

Throughout the Union weavers were suffering similar experiences. A thriving trade in weaving coarse linens and cambrics had once existed in Derryhirk. In early 1847, however, it was reported, 'by that employment now a large majority of the families could not earn more than three shillings for the week'.

Moira weavers were said to be undergoing 'unmitigated hardship' and were now 'deeply plunged into misery'. Three types of weaving constituted the industrial basis of that area – linens, cambric and damask-diaper. Weavers of the latter were comparatively well-off, earning between ten and fifteen shillings per week. However, others were not as fortunate:

> The occasions are rare in which a cambric weaver can earn more than three or four shillings a week. The linen weaver is even worse for his tenure of employment is frequently more fluctuating... being unable to obtain yarn.[14]

In the Bleary area, a writer reported seeing weavers' families 'sitting listless by the remains of an apology for a fire – without work, means of food, their children famished with cold and hunger'.[15]

Obtaining accurate data relating to such hardship can prove difficult. However, one source that does remain is that of pawn-shop returns.

In Tartaraghan the poor were reported to have 'almost entirely sold or pawned their clothes – even in many cases sold their Bible – having no further resources from whence to draw'.[16] From Bleary one report stated:

> To dream of finding furniture in the houses of the poor in this district would be folly. There is no such thing; all has gone for food.[17]

Likewise in Moira a labourer's house was found to be in a similar condition:

There was not in the entire abode half-a-crown's worth of furniture; in fact it was about as desolate a looking shelter as any I have yet come across. Everything they had possessed was sold for whatever it would bring to 'keep the life in the children'.[18]

The *Banner of Ulster* gave the following report of the tenants living on the Marquis of Hertford's estate in Ballinderry:

There are small farmers on the estate who have already sold the best part of their livestock to meet current expenses – the future will be mortgaged to provide for the present. The labour of next year will be put in pawn to pay the losses of this season.[19]

For many, then, pawning their belongings was the only hope of obtaining money on credit. In Lurgan there were four pawn shops, while Portadown had three. An analysis of their transactions in the years 1845-7 is given in Table 9 and this confirms the patterns noted above.

Table 9: Pawnshop returns, 1844-47

	1844	1845	1846	1847
No. of Articles				
LURGAN	59,683	86,834	122,301	33,473
PORTADOWN	48,544	59,489	55,880	37,539
Amount Lent (£s)				
LURGAN	8,720	13,235	16,252	4,889
PORTADOWN	3,103	5,181	3,816	2,030

Source: Papers relating to Proceedings for the Relief of Distress and state of Unions and Workhouses in Ireland, H.C., 1849, (1042) Vol. xlviii, p. 156.

1846 saw a substantial increase in the numbers of items pawned as compared with the previous year; yet their value was just over £1,500 more, suggesting that many small and worthless items were pawned in a time of need.

However, in 1847, total items pawned represented less than one half of that of the previous year – supporting the hypothesis that the poor had indeed pawned or sold everything they had, in order to survive. Consequently one pawn shop in Lurgan closed, probably due to lack of business and little or no return on items pawned.

Some in their hopelessness turned to crime to obtain food. However, attacks on boats and barges near Portadown represented only one aspect of a general rise in crime in the Famine period. As the following figures illustrate, both crimes and convictions showed a marked rise in 1847 as compared with previous years.

Table 10: Crimes and convictions in Co. Armagh, 1844-47

| Year | Co. Armagh | |
	Crimes committed	Convictions
	Number	
1844	513	244
1845	396	189
1846	452	267
1847	764	474

Source: Thom's Irish Almanac and Official Directory, 1849, p. 200

The papers abounded with court cases relating to theft of flax, linen-yarn, food and animals. The problems were such that William Verner wrote to the local Clerk of the Peace, to demand that an increased number of policemen be sent from Lurgan to Derrycorry:

> Their presence in that locality is much needed as outrages are of nightly occurrence, and the farmers have to sit up at night to guard their property.[20]

He related how

> a cow was killed and carried away on Sunday night last and our endeavours to discover the perpetrators of these acts without the assistance of the police are perfectly useless.[21]

The reasons for such a marked increase in crime were commented upon by a local police constable:

> At the sessions of Lurgan there was an increase of offences ranging under the charge of larceny compared with the last sessions, which I attribute without the least hesitation to the

universal destitution which obtains here. The population of
this county suffers under the privations of this season in as great
a degree as the population of the south; but either a greater
power of endurance, or a general respect for the laws, has caused
an abstinence from any serious attack on property; although a
continuance of such conduct under increasing distress may be
very problematical.[22]

Given these manifestations of despair and destitution we may
wonder as to the reaction of the local landed gentry, many of
whom were resident in the area.

Figure 24: Brownlow House, home of Lord Lurgan

The many tributes paid to Lord Lurgan on the occasion of his
death suggest that he was held in very high regard. Each press
report commented on his concern for the welfare of his tenants
and much of this praise appears warranted. As Chairman of both
the Lurgan Board of Guardians and the Lurgan Relief Committee,
he made generous contributions not only to the Lurgan Relief
Fund but to similar funds in Drumcree and Tartaraghan. The
Northern Whig reported before his death in April how Lord Lurgan,
together with his wife, attended the 'Belfast Bazaar for the relief
of destitution' to which they both contributed donations and made
'extensive purchases'.[23]

Meanwhile in Moira, the Rev. Wynne, together with others, offered to voluntarily tax themselves threepence in the pound. Sir Robert Bateson agreed to match any sum raised by this method. The tax elicited a total of £90 and Bateson made this up to a total of £180. This was then used to establish a soup kitchen in the village. For his part James Brown, a Donaghcloney linen bleacher, donated twenty-five guineas to the local soup kitchen and was reported to 'regularly dispense from half-a-crown to five shillings daily in casual charity'. Indeed in 1850 Brown made a contribution to the building of the Catholic chapel in Clare despite not being a member of that faith.

However, Brown's generosity and goodwill, particularly during the Famine, was not evident amongst many of his peers. One source noted this when stating:

> Here is an example which is worthy of being remembered and followed by some whose properties reach our own doors, and who revel in the receipt of incomes forty times larger than that of Mr. Brown.[24]

The criticism levelled by the Rev. Clements at landlords in Tartaraghan has already been noted. The rector was not alone in finding the gentry difficult to deal with. David Babbington revealed that all the landlords in Drumcree were absentee and had contributed nothing to relief. Only Thomas Wakefield, a small landowner, had made an attempt to provide support. At a relief meeting in Seagoe Parish Church on 4th January 1847, the Rev. James Saurin, Chairman of the Seagoe Relief Committee, informed the gathering of his lack of success in obtaining support for fund-raising from local landlords:

> From the proprietors of Kernan – Messrs. Moore and Bullock – I received no answer to my application. From two of the proprietors of Edenderry – Dean Adams and Mr. Atkinson – I received a refusal. From no other landed proprietor in the district did I receive any communication ... save from Mr. James Robinson of Levaghery, who forwarded a contribution of £1.[25]

It later emerged that Atkinson had contributed to that portion of his land under the auspices of the Portadown Relief Fund. He refused, however, to contribute to the area under the Seagoe fund. For his part, Dean Adams revealed that as he had recently transferred his land holding in Seagoe to his son, he was not liable to make a contribution. The Rev. Saurin treated this excuse with contempt:

> I thought the landlord who had, to my knowledge, enjoyed the hard earnings of a poor set of tenants, for upwards of twenty years, was better entitled, were it only on a principle of gratitude, to contribute in their hour of necessity, a modicum of twenty years income, than that son of his who had, according to your own showing, not only just come into possession, but had never received one farthing out of the property. Permit me, farther, to say, whilst you were the proprietor, though repeatedly applied to, I never was able to induce you to contribute one shilling towards the relief of the paupers on your property.[26]

The indifference of Dean Adams was in stark contrast to the endeavours of local clergymen of all denominations who laboured tirelessly to alleviate widespread destitution. Each relief committee had at least one cleric at the helm; for example, the Rev. Oulton and Fr. O'Brien in Lurgan, the Rev. Babbington in Drumcree, the Rev. Mulligan in Magheralin, and the Rev. Wynne in Moira. Many more offered their services and it is quite ironic therefore to find one prominent landlord more interested in the spiritual welfare of his tenants.

In a report on 7th January 1847, the *Northern Whig* informed its readers of a society having been formed,

> to raise a large sum of money to be applied in consequence of the present famine, not to feed the hungry and revive those fainting from want, but to make proselytes, taking advantage of the existing calamity.[27]

The society itself, in an advertisement, described the hunger and fever as 'this present favourable crisis which must not be allowed to pass unimproved'. It believed that an opportunity had now arisen to bring the Bible into 'the unenlightened portions of the people' whilst also maintaining that openings had been found 'which in ordinary times are sought in vain'. In conclusion it informed its readers that a committee of 'noblemen and gentlemen' had been formed in order to raise £20,000 to further its objective. The first signatory to this appeal was the Duke of

Manchester, owner of eight townlands in Kernan and holding much more land around Tandragee. Although he made contributions to the Seagoe/Kernan Relief Fund, these totalled less than half those made by the Rev. Saurin. Unlike Lord Lurgan, then, the Duke's contribution to relief in Seagoe was minimal. Hence, it is difficult to argue with the *Northern Whig's* assertion that

> the Duke was too much taken up with the spiritual concerns of the famished poor to have time or inclination to look to their physical condition.[28]

Figure 25: The Venerable James Saurin, Archdeacon of Dromore and Rector of Seagoe, 1826-1879

Another newspaper, the *Banner of Ulster*, accused the proprietors of Ballydougan – Mrs. Whittle and Miss Wallace of Dublin – of exhibiting 'supreme heartlessness and most niggardly generosity towards the poor'. Although they had given money to all their poorer tenantry in order to purchase seed oats, this action was described as representing 'not a tithe of what is necessary for purposes essentially requisite'. The report concluded thus:

> A £40 subscription from the absentee drawer of hundreds and hundreds of pounds yearly, in a time of famine, is but a mockery of charity. At the same time, the owners are living in fashionable luxury, dreaming, no doubt, that their mite is the means of saving the poor from regular depopulation.[29]

Another landlord who appeared indifferent to the suffering of his tenants was Charles Douglass of Grace Hall, Moira. He was the Chairman of the Magheralin Relief Committee and yet on 23 September, 1847 he seized 480 stooks of oats for rent and arrears of rent due to him on the lands of Ballymacbredan.[30] This action hardly appears that of one concerned about local distress.

A similar example of insensitivity comes from the minute book of the Portadown Market Company. In June 1847, three sheds at the market were being used as a soup kitchen and this caused annoyance to the committee. They were worried that the numbers of paupers availing of the charity would deter customers. Hence they demanded that action be taken, recommending that 'said soup kitchen and all things connected therewith be removed... permanently'.

The human tragedy of this situation was exemplified by the condition of one of the paupers who attended the kitchen. Mary Campbell, along with two children, 'was attending at the soup kitchen for relief and lay down. She has been lying there for the last ten days'. This woman, like many others, was suffering from fever. What was the reaction of local businessmen?

> By direction of Mr. Woodhouse, Richard Casey applied to Mr. Willis to get this woman removed, but he declined. Doing so Mr. Casey also applied to Mr. May as Guardian of the Poor to have her removed, which he undertook to do. He afterwards neglected to do so but he got a shilling from Mr. Woodhouse for the purpose.[31]

In this case hard-headed businessmen were not prepared to tolerate either a soup kitchen or a sick woman interfering with their potential for profit.

Figure 26: Carrick Blacker House, home of Col. Blacker

It may be argued that the gentry lived their lives apart from those in poverty, whose houses were often crammed together up long country lanes well out of sight of the main roads. Thus, manifestations of the misery then rampant would have been kept to a minimum. However, as the previous examples have shown, some members of the business and gentry class appeared indifferent to such suffering. For those genuinely interested in the plight of the poor, such scenes could not be ignored. In 1847 James Stuart sent Indian meal from New York to the value of £4 to be distributed amongst the poor by members of Donaghcloney Presbyterian Church.[32] Thus, the sorrowful tales from home provoked a person, thousands of miles away, to help as best he could.

Some who worked among the poor were so distressed by what they witnessed that they could not accept it any longer, as the following report from the Moravian Church in Ballinderry in July 1847 illustrates.

> Mr. B. Davis suddenly left his post for Bristol without acquainting anyone of his intention. He states his reason by letter afterwards, that his heart was almost broken by witnessing the distress of the poor Irish. He could obtain no comfort or rest day or night and he felt himself unequal to the duties he had undertaken.[33]

Figure 27: Manor House, home of John Hancock

However, for the business class and the gentry, life went on as normal throughout this period of distress. Agricultural fairs were held in early 1847 in Charlestown, Maghery, Moira and Lurgan. On 22 February the Lurgan Union Farming Society held a ploughing match at Kilmore which drew an attendance of over two thousand people. The *Newry Telegraph* reported the occasion as follows:

> The ploughing match was most creditable... and an extensive prospect of the rich and fertile counties of Down, Antrim and Armagh could not but cause the beholder to compare it with

the desolation of the South and acknowledge that only in our
own happy Ulster could the like be found.[34]

It appears to have been overlooked by this reporter that in this
part of his 'happy Ulster', 516 people had died within three months
in the local workhouse.

The same society held another show in September at which
were exhibited 'superior breeds' of cattle, pigs, poultry, together
with green crops. Afterwards, the members retired to the
Brownlow Arms Hotel to enjoy 'an excellent and substantial
dinner.' This comfortable upper-class lifestyle is further attested
to by the fact that Messrs. Greer, Hancock and Douglass, together
with their families, were able to travel on annual holidays to
France in the mid-1840s.[35]

At the same time, Colonel Blacker, in his diary, lists journeys
to Frankfurt, Paris, Brussels and London between 1845 and 1847.[36]

Mixing in such circles, it is perhaps not surprising that to some
of these people, the distress being suffered by the poor would
have been regarded as little more than an irritant or
embarrassment. Newspapers such as the *Armagh Guardian* and
Newry Telegraph reflected this outlook. They were more interested
in informing their readership of British colonial wars in Africa
and India or high politics in Europe and America, rather than in
addressing the widespread destitution then confronting them.
To have done the latter, of course, would almost inevitably have
involved criticising Boards of Guardians and relief methods. This
was to be avoided at all costs – both papers refused to publish a
letter severely critical of the Lurgan Guardians and the local Relief
Committee. The same letter, quoted earlier, was published by
the anti-establishment *Belfast Vindicator*, and proved to be a
valuable contribution to understanding the problems in this area.

There is little doubt that the actions of all those involved in
relief activities were severely constricted by the rigorous
enforcement of the Poor Law. As stated in Chapter one, this was
vigorously opposed by local landowners as it represented the
imposition of a new tax. Thus, most of the petitions against it
focussed on this particular aspect of the measure. An interesting

variation appeared in a petition from the parishioners of Kilmore, later part of the Armagh Union:

> Your Petitioners are convinced that the principle on which the Bill is founded, namely the confinement of the poor in workhouses, is totally incompatible with the disposition and habits of the Irish people ... as it punishes pauperism as a crime, inflicting on the poor imprisonment, scanty subsistence, rigorous discipline and hard labour.[37]

However, government ideology of the time ignored such arguments, believing that poverty resulted not from genuine need, but from laziness and indolence on the part of the poor themselves. Thus, they were to be punished for it – the workhouses were the embodiment of this ethos. Such a system was unlikely to provide the relief measures required during a disaster on the scale of the Famine. Nevertheless, with the exception of the implementation of the Temporary Relief Act in May 1847, the Poor Law, together with the workhouses, was the major source of relief for thousands who, under normal circumstances, would not have had recourse to it.

Those responsible for the poor under the law were, of course, the local Board of Guardians, both elected and ex officio. To them fell the task of appointing workhouse officials, selecting a medical officer and tendering for contracts. It could be argued that the election of Guardians, together with that of local Town Commissioners, symbolised the first steps towards representative democracy in Ireland in the nineteenth century. As such, these men – there were no women – were relatively inexperienced at this stage and hence judgments made in hindsight are unfair. However, the fact remains that the Lurgan workhouse was one of the worst such institutions in Ulster – surpassed in its inefficiency only by those Unions in Connacht and Munster which had their local Guardians replaced by government-appointed vice-Guardians.

An examination of attendance by the Guardians demonstrates, to a large degree, why the workhouse encountered serious problems in 1847. While men such as Cuppage, Hancock and McCarten appeared to have had a genuine interest in the plight of the poor, many of their contemporaries appeared indifferent. Between March 1846 and March 1847, only 11 of the 32 Guardians attended more than 50 of the 52 meetings held. Indeed, only three attended 40 meetings or more. Such apathy offers clues as to the apparent indifference of the Guardians in relation to the suffering in the workhouse, their incompetence in appointing and dealing with officials and contractors, and the general ineptitude in the everyday running of the workhouse.

Figure 28: Grace Hall, home of Charles Douglass

Yet these same men, at the rate-in-aid meetings two years later, were both vociferous and vindictive in their criticism of administrators in the West and South. For a group of people who had overseen a catastrophe in their own area, they showed no mercy, no understanding and no willingness to admit of their own shortcomings in 1847. Unlike the West and South, they had only to contend with one year of serious distress. The former witnessed at least five successive years whereby their population was decimated. If it had not been for the revival of the linen industry in 1848, this area could well have suffered equal devastation.

The neglect and incompetence of those charged with administering the Union resulted in the deaths of 1,245 people in the workhouse in 1847. Such a calamity cannot be pushed to one side as representing mistakes on the part of inexperienced and overburdened Guardians. Doubtless, the influx of huge numbers of paupers in the winter of 1846-7 was not expected and the workhouse officials were overwhelmed by the demands for relief. However, neighbouring administrations in Banbridge and Armagh had faced similar problems and managed to cope without the huge mortality levels witnessed in Lurgan. As the following years illustrated, with deaths reduced to 348 in 1848 and 227 in 1849, sensible administration and careful planning could have ensured that deaths in 1847, although inevitable, would have been much reduced.

Although unfair to apportion blame to any individual, it was clear that Dr. Bell was not capable of dealing with the huge task confronting him. His shortcomings as a medical officer had been exposed in early 1846, yet the Guardians, unable to read the signs, and apparently heedless to problems already manifesting themselves in other parts of the country, insisted on maintaining him in his post. Dr. Smith's subsequent scathing indictment of the workhouse, together with the inquiry into food, demonstrated how the Guardians had made an art form out of 'turning a blind eye'. Indeed, in 1841, Henry John Porter, moral agent of the Duke of Manchester, wrote to the workhouse as follows:

> The state of the workhouse, both as regards classification and cleanliness, is very imperfect... Various parts of the house are not washed more than once a week instead of every day as at Banbridge and other Union workhouses – and many parts of the house are not washed so often as once a week.[38]

Little wonder then that six years later Fr. O'Brien could report finding the body of a man which had lain undiscovered in a ward for 16 hours.[39] It was this 'dereliction of duty' which ensured that the workhouse was more akin to a morgue than a place of respite in 1847.

Although the workhouse was the focus of relief efforts in the Union, distress was widespread. An analysis of church records for this period reveals the extent of suffering in these years. Appendix B details mortality levels in the period 1840-50. By establishing the average numbers of deaths for each year from 1840-6, we can gauge the level of 'excess mortality' in 1847, i.e. the number of deaths above and beyond those which would have naturally occurred in that year. The information is somewhat skewed as there remain much better records for the Church of Ireland than any other congregation. Allowing for such shortcomings, the analysis is nevertheless valuable. Parishes of all denominations suffered 942 'excess deaths' in that year, with the Church of Ireland congregations in Drumcree, Seagoe and Shankill, together with the Catholic parishes of Tullylish and Seagoe, suffering particularly badly. For the period 1848-9 the level of 'excess mortality' dropped to 133, giving a total of 1,075 deaths. This figure, combined with the 'excess mortality' in the workhouse of 1,848, gives an overall total of 2,933 excess deaths in the Lurgan Union for the period 1846-9.

Most of the deaths occurred as a result of typhus or relapsing fever, both of which were highly contagious. Lack of proper food, such as uncooked Indian meal, also occasioned mortality by dysentery or chronic diarrhoea, whilst the cholera epidemic of 1849 claimed more than 130 victims. This pattern was repeated throughout the country, with deaths by actual starvation accounting for a relatively small percentage of the total; however, there were cases of such deaths in Lurgan, Tartaraghan and Bleary.

An increase in deaths is perhaps an obvious consequence of famine in any area. Interestingly though, the church records reveal significant data in relation to birth rates. Using the same technique as that for mortality levels, we find that 1847 witnessed 580 'averted births', i.e. the number that, on average, could have normally been expected. For the period 1847-9 as a whole, the figure is 470, emphasising the point that the Famine represented an all-embracing social catastrophe, resulting both in huge mortality levels and a significant decline in the birth rate.

Such were the consequences of 'this dreadful visitation' in the Lurgan Union in the 1840s. Given that approximately one-third of the local population relied almost exclusively on the potato, it is not surprising to find that they were hardest hit by the blight. However, those previously regarded as exempt from such dangers, the linen weavers, were themselves drawn into the web of hunger and disease as a consequence of a serious slump in the linen industry in 1847-8. This, together with sub-standard flax and oats crops, accompanied by a huge rise in the price of provisions, ensured that the Famine wreaked havoc in this area.

Those operating local relief committees, aided by the Quakers, were indefatigable in their efforts to provide aid. However, the local gentry, with only a couple of exceptions, appeared aloof, cold and distant from the tragedy unfolding before them.

For their part, the Board of Guardians, together with the officials they employed, were at best incompetent, at worst negligent in their attempts to deal with the huge numbers of famine-stricken paupers pleading for relief. It is perhaps ironic, then, that the legacy of their neglect, like the paupers who relied on them for their survival, has been buried without trace for one hundred and fifty years.

Footnotes

1. William Blacker to Dr Kane, 10 December 1845, Relief Commission Papers, (N.A).
2. Reports from Assistant Handloom Weavers' Commissioners, Part III, p. 714, H.C. 1840 (220) XXIII.
3. W. H. Crawford, *The Handloom Weavers and the Ulster Linen Industry*, Ulster Historical Foundation, 1994, pp. 51-63.
4. Reports from Assistant Handloom Weavers' Commissioners, Part III, p. 644, H.C. 1840, (220) XXIII.
5. P. Ollerenshaw , 'Industry, 1820-1914', in L Kennedy and P Ollerenshaw (ed) *An Economic History of Ulster 1820-1939*, Manchester University Press, 1985, p. 76.

6. P. Mathias, *The First Industrial Nation – An Economic History of Britain 1700-1914,* Methuen, 1983, p. 258.
7. P. Ollerenshaw, 'Industry 1820-1914', p. 76.
8. *Northern Whig,* 22 May 1847.
9. *Belfast News Letter,* 25 May, 1848.
10. *Northern Whig,* 20 March 1847.
11. *Ibid.* 17 May 1847.
12. The Transactions of the Central Relief Committee of the Society of Friends during the Famine in Ireland in 1846 and 1847, Appendix III, p 191.
13. *Ibid.* p. 192.
14. *Banner of Ulster,* 2 March 1847.
15. *Ibid.* 12th February, 1847.
16. The Transactions of the Central Relief Committee of the Society of Friends during the Famine in Ireland in 1846 and 1847, Appendix III, p. 192.
17. *Banner of Ulster,* 12th February, 1847.
18. *Ibid.* 16th February, 1847.
19. *Ibid.* 27th November, 1846.
20. William Verner to Leonard Dobbin, 21 January 1847, Outrage Papers.
21. *Ibid.* 21 January 1847
22. Report of W. Millar, Portadown, 20 January 1847, Outrage Papers.
23. *Northern Whig,* 6th April 1847.

Bibliography

1. Manuscript sources

National Archives, Dublin

    Constabulary Returns 1845-6.
    Distress Papers 1846-7.
    Outrage Papers 1846-7.
    Relief Commission Papers 1845-7.

Public Record Office, Belfast

    Lurgan Union Board of Guardians' Minute Books 1839-48 BG22/A.
    Indoor Workhouse Registers 1841-8 BG22/G.
    Workhouse Chaplains' Report Books 1846-8 BG22/FO.
    Letter Book of John Hancock D1817/2.
    Lurgan Town Commissioners' Minute Book 1846 LA51/2B/2.
    Portadown Market Company Minute Book 1847 4A64/21AA/1.
    Workhouse Outward Letter Book 1840-4 BG22/B.

Armagh County Museum

    The Blacker Day Books - The Diaries of Col. William Blacker.

Craigavon Heritage Office

    Minute Book of Portadown Mont de Piétè Society, 1844-7.

Shankill Parish Church, Lurgan

    Burial Register of Church of Ireland, Shankill, 1845-7.

2. Printed Contemporary Records

Annual Reports of The Poor Law Commissioners, 1838-48.
The Dublin Almanac and General Register of Ireland, 1847.
Thom's Irish Almanac and Official Directory, 1849.
Transactions of the Central Relief Committee of the Society of Friends
    during the Famine in Ireland in 1846 and 1847.
Parliamentary Gazetteer of Ireland, vol. ii, 1846.

3. Newspapers

    Armagh Guardian
    Belfast News Letter
    Belfast Vindicator
    Newry Telegraph
    Northern Whig

4. British Parliamentary Papers

First Report of Commissioners for Inquiring into the condition of the
    Poorer Classes in Ireland. Supplement to Appendix D. H.C., 1836,
    Vol. XXXI; Supplement to Appendix E. H.C., 1836, Vol. XXXII.

Reports from Assistant Handloom Weavers' Commissioners. H.C., 1840, (220), Vol. XXIII.

Report from Commissioners of Inquiry into the Law and Practice in Respect to the Occupation of Land in Ireland, The Devon Commission. Digest of Evidence, Part 1. H.C., 1845 (605) Vol. XIX.

Report to the Board of Health, Dublin, on the State of the Lurgan Union Workhouse, by Dr Smith. H.C., 1847, (257), Vol. LV. ii.

Correspondence relating to the state of the Union Workhouses in Ireland. H.C., 1847, (863), Vol. LV.

Third Report from the Relief Commissioners. H.C., 1847, (836), Vol. XVII.

Fourth Report from the Relief Commissioners. H.C., 1847, (859), Vol. XVIII.

Fifth Report from the Relief Commissioners. H.C., 1847-8, (876), Vol. XXIX.

Agricultural Returns for the year 1847. H.C., 1847-8, (923), Vol. LVii.

Papers Relating to Proceedings for the Relief of Distress and state of Unions and Workhouses in Ireland. H.C., 1849, (1042),Vol. XLVIII.

5. Secondary Sources

Campbell, F., *The Dissenting Voice - Protestant Democracy in Ulster from Plantation to Partition.* Blackstaff Press, 1991.

Connell, P., *Changing Forces Shaping a Nineteenth-Century Irish Town: A Case Study of Navan.* Occasional Papers, No. 1, Maynooth, 1978.

Crawford, W. H., *The Handloom Weavers and the Ulster Linen Industry.* Ulster Historical Foundation, 1994.

Durnin, P., *Derry and the Irish Poor Law - A History of the Derry Workhouse.* The Waterside Community Local History Group, 1991.

Evans, E. E. (ed.) *Harvest Home, the Last Sheaf: A Selection from the Writings of T.G.F. Patterson,* Dundalk, Dundalgan Press, 1975.

Farrell, M., *The Poor Law and the Workhouse in Belfast 1838-1948.* P.R.O.N.I. 1978.

Green, E. R. R., *The Lagan Valley 1800-50 - A Local History of the Industrial Revolution.* Faber and Faber Ltd, 1949.

Kane, J. *For God and the King,* Lurgan, Ulster Society, 1995.

Kennedy, L. and Ollerenshaw, P.(eds.) *An Economic History of Ulster 1820 -1940.* Manchester University Press, 1985.

Kinealy, C., *This Great Calamity, The Irish Famine 1845-52.* Gill and MacMillan, 1994.

McCorry, F. X., *Lurgan: An Irish Provincial Town 1610-1970.* Inglewood Press, 1993.

Mathias, P., *The First Industrial Nation - An Economic History of Britain 1700-1914.* Methuen, 1983.

O'Connor, J., *The Workhouses of Ireland - The Fate of Ireland's Poor.* Anvil Books, 1995.

Appendix A

Lurgan Workhouse Admissions by electoral division
1 January - 31 December 1847

Aghagallon	118
Aghalee	21
Ballinderry	31
Ballyleny	20
Breagh	152
Brownlowsderry	103
Carrowbrack	121
Cornakinnegar	102
Donaghcloney	103
Drumcree	253
Kernan	108
Lurgan	492
Magheralin	73
Moira	69
Montiaghs	89
Portadown	314
Tartaraghan	157
Tullylish	383
Waringstown	165
Union at large	393

Appendix B
Church Records

Burials per Year

Church of Ireland

	1840	1841	1842	1843	1844	1845	1846	1847	1848	1849	1850
Aghalee	49	53	47	45	65	52	65	91	41	39	41
Ballinderry	35	32	32	16	33	24	39	53	22	32	21
Donaghcloney	30	33	27	22	35	27	29	46	40	n.k.	22
Drumcree	143	100	85	107	132	80	78	388	136	95	76
Magheralin	40	51	36	59	58	41	55	74	67	62	47
Moira	11	17	11	9	13	9	9	22	12	4	12
Montiaghs	6	6	8	4	2	2	6	22	5	12	9
Seagoe	59	51	45	50	49	44	67	108	58	52	43
Tartaraghan	32	36	23	42	36	30	51	89	36	34	24
Shankill	78	69	52	93	68	81	102	492*	151	80	67

*includes 233 workhouse deaths

Catholic

	1840	1841	1842	1843	1844	1845	1846	1847	1848	1849	1850
Magheralin	26	25	27	5	12	8	17	22	34	39	20
Seagoe	42	34	33	34	30	36	44	165	42	30	23
Tullylish	22	34	44	22	n.k.	n.k.	33	120	71	47	70

Baptisms per year

					Church of Ireland						
	1840	1841	1842	1843	1844	1845	1846	1847	1848	1849	1850
Aghalee	92	127	153	91	96	98	102	60	70	80	75
Drumcree	97	117	93	154	124	153	122	62	48	118	112
Knocknamuckly	35	38	35	63	66	75	98	28	58	62	97
Magheralin	98	78	84	112	115	114	96	90	88	111	129
Milltown	7	37	34	31	44	66	48	30	24	40	49
Moira	55	56	75	55	50	59	53	53	46	43	51
Montiaghs	n.k.	n.k.	3	23	21	30	28	9	18	23	18
Portadown	42	40	104	106	92	72	51	26	39	44	49
Seagoe	120	138	107	134	157	139	136	99	72	129	116
Shankill	97	124	130	135	153	162	176	129	133	168	183
Tartaraghan	78	70	78	79	89	99	121	66	61	62	85
Tullylish	73	110	153	123	158	122	116	79	n.k.	124	n.k.

Catholic

	1840	1841	1842	1843	1844	1845	1846	1847	1848	1849	1850
Lurgan	124	165	135	143	152	159	117	88	39	83	116
Magheralin	78	69	94	43	55	51	85	55	64	65	75
Seagoe	124	131	162	134	143	160	153	67	96	121	136
Tartaraghan	162	139	177	158	131	139	104	103	62	94	100

Methodist

	1840	1841	1842	1843	1844	1845	1846	1847	1848	1849	1850
Portadown	48	40	31	40	30	27	31	24	23	29	21
Lurgan	10	19	18	23	25	24	10	8	17	18	16

Presbyterian

	1840	1841	1842	1843	1844	1845	1846	1847	1848	1849	1850
Lurgan	60	85	75	71	70	52	33	28	26	27	28
Portadown	13	4	10	6	8	9	11	6	13	8	6

Appendix C

Lurgan Workhouse Admissions per month, January 1845 - December 1849

	1845	1846	1847	1848	1849
January	49	119	480	533	230
February	43	130	37	343	191
March	51	133	178	274	178
April	28	157	28	238	181
May	48	137	267	211	224
June	39	141	341	183	219
July	44	65	315	99	164
August	37	80	203	113	108
September	19	126	263	123	65
October	38	230	340	158	75
November	41	270	413	264	124
December	29	597	572	306	106

Appendix D

The Quaker Relief Scheme

Many relief organisations helped to relieve distress in the Lurgan Union. Most of the aid was in the form of money, although, on occasions, blankets and clothes were also supplied. Little has been said of the important role played by the Society of Friends (Quakers) in such relief. The visits by members of the Society throughout the country and locally in Tartaraghan, emphasised the need for a systematic relief effort by them.

It is generally assumed that most Quaker relief took place in areas such as Mayo, Clare and Cork, with little aid finding its way North. However, substantial aid was forthcoming for the Lurgan/Portadown area, in the form of money, clothing and food, usually from a central relief depot in Belfast.

Given the logistics involved in establishing and running a huge distribution effort, the Central Relief Committee of the Society of Friends took great pains in establishing the particular needs of those areas applying for relief.

Application forms detailing the level of relief already available in certain districts had to be completed before any action could be taken. Thus, for example, when the Rev. Oulton applied, he received the following reply on 21 April, 1847:

> The Committee cannot with propriety assist a body having such a large relief fund. If assistance should hereafter really be needed, we will be willing to grant it.

Fr. Edward Mulligan of Magheralin also received a rebuff in July of the same year, being informed that:

> The means at the disposal of this Committee do not admit of their making general grants in aid to those destitute classes of persons for whom legislative provision is made.

Similarly, the Committee also placed conditions on supplies of aid. On 24 April 1847 one ton of Indian meal was ordered to be delivered to Archdeacon Saurin to be distributed amongst those 'who are not included under new assistance (the Temporary Relief Act)'. On May 13 Rev. Oulton received half a ton of meal and seven bags of rice for distribution 'in a cooked state to such poor children at school as may request it'.

The Quakers were determined to ensure that the aid was not tainted with charges of proselytism and religious favouritism. Thus, when George Hamilton of Castle Lane, Lurgan was supplied with one ton of Indian meal, the Committee specified that the Wesleyan relief committee supply it 'to the destitute of all religious professions'.

In this way the Quaker relief scheme was made available to all religious persuasions throughout the Union in 1847 and 1848. The following tables indicate the extent of that aid and emphasise the point that distress in this area continued into 1848, even though 1847 was the worst year in terms of fatalities.

Grants of Money

DATE	GRANTEE	AREA	AMOUNT
26/ 1/47	David Babbington	Drumcree	£20
20/ 2/47	Jacob Green	Trummery, Moira	£15.14.8
1/ 3/47	Francis Clements	Tartaraghan	£30
29/ 3/47	Edward Mulligan	Magheralin	£30
17/ 4/47	Jacob Green	Trummery, Moira	£30
18/12/47	Mary M. Uprichard	Fairview, Lurgan	£13.10.0
27/ 5/47	Charles Wakefield	Portadown	£25

Clothing Grants

DATE	GRANTEE	AREA	GRANT
20.1.48	David Babbington	Drumcree	No. 1, omitting garments, blue print, leather and fustian
3.4.48	Francis Clements	Tartaraghan	No. 1, omitting rugs and sheets
8.12.48	Jacob Green	Trummery, Moira	56 garments, 1 pair grey calico, 1 pair blue print, 1 flannel, 1 fustian, 20 bed rugs, 5 pairs cotton sheets, 1 bale leather
12.12.48	Elizabeth Wakefield	Moyallen	1 pair corduroy, 1 pair fustian, 1 pair flannel, 1 pair calico, 12 rugs, 6 pairs sheets, 3 grey frocks, 60 garments, 5 coats, 12 waistcoats, 2 quilts, 2 blankets, 10 chemises, 1 gown
n.d.	Jacob Green	Trummery, Moira	2 pairs calico, 1 flannel, 1 corduroy, 1 check, 1 bale leather, 12 shawls, 6 coats, 4 shirts, 6 dresses, 2 child's dresses, 2 petticoats, 20 pairs hose
n.d.	Mary Uprichard	Fairview, Lurgan	2 pairs grey calico, 1 pair fustian, 1 doz. guernsey frocks, 1 doz. worsted frocks, 1 band cotton, 2 blue print
n.d.	Anne Wakefield & Ann Babbington	Portadown	6 coats, 6 pairs men's trousers, 4 men's vests, 4 boys' vests, 2 worsted dresses, 6 bedgowns, 3 boys' capes, 18 children's dresses, 24 girls' & women's chemises, 2 pairs sheets, 4 cloaks, 12 shirts, 30 children's coats, 2 pairs flannel, 6 wollen capes, 7 boy's capes, 2 guernsey frocks, 2 boys' jackets, 2 pairs gaiters, 50 girls' & women's petticoats, 2 girls' coats, 2 men's smocks, 2 men's capes, 2 pairs men's trousers

The No. 1 Grant referred to in the table above consisted of:

10 Guernsey frocks	1 pair corduroy
2 pairs grey calico	10 pairs rugs
2 pairs blue print	10 pairs sheets
1 pair flannel	1 bale leather
1 pair fustian	

Grants of Food

DATE	GRANTEE	AREA	GRANT
24.4.47	Simon Foot	Knocknamuckley	1 ton rice
24.4.47	George Hamilton	Castle Lane, Lurgan	1 ton Indian meal
28.4.47	James Saurin	Kernan	1 ton Indian meal
5.5.47	Fred Cashel	Churchview, Tartaraghan	$1/_2$ ton rice
13.5.47	Rev. Wm. Oulton	Lurgan	$1/_2$ ton meal, 7 bags rice
15.5.47	Charles Wakefield	Portadown	$1/_2$ ton East Indian rice, 2 tons Carolina rice, 28lb ginger
26.5.47	Mary Uprichard	Fairview, Lurgan	$1/_2$ ton rice
29.5.47	Rev. Wm. Oulton	Lurgan	$1/_2$ ton Indian meal, 7 bags of rice
2.6.47	Fanny Cuppage	Silverwood, Lurgan	5cwt Indian meal, 5cwt wheaten meal
19.6.47	David Babbington	Drumcree	1 ton rice, 1 boiler
23.6.47	Henry Willis	Portadown	1 ton rice
14.7.47	George Hamilton	Castle Lane, Lurgan	1 ton Indian meal

Index